What the Citizen Should Know

OUR ARMS AND WEAPONS

What the Citizen

Should Know About

OUR ARMS

AND WEAPONS

A Guide to
Weapons
from the
1940s

JAMES E. HICKS

MAJOR, ORDNANCE DEPARTMENT,
ARMY OF THE UNITED STATES

Illustrations by André Jandôt

Skyhorse Publishing

First Published in 1941
First Skyhorse Publishing edition 2015

All rights reserved. No part of this book may be reproduced in any manner without the express written consent of the publisher, except in the case of brief excerpts in critical reviews or articles. All inquiries should be addressed to Skyhorse Publishing, 307 West 36th Street, 11th Floor, New York, NY 10018.

Skyhorse Publishing books may be purchased in bulk at special discounts for sales promotion, corporate gifts, fund-raising, or educational purposes. Special editions can also be created to specifications. For details, contact the Special Sales Department, Skyhorse Publishing, 307 West 36th Street, 11th Floor, New York, NY 10018 or info@skyhorsepublishing.com.

Skyhorse® and Skyhorse Publishing® are registered trademarks of Skyhorse Publishing, Inc.®, a Delaware corporation.

Visit our website at www.skyhorsepublishing.com.

10 9 8 7 6 5 4 3 2 1

Library of Congress Cataloging-in-Publication Data is available on file.

Cover design by Owen Corrigan
Cover photo credit: Thinkstock

Print ISBN: 978-1-63220-278-9

Printed in China

CONTENTS

LIST OF ILLUSTRATIONS

ACKNOWLEDGMENTS

———

THE author wishes to thank Mr. André Jandôt for executing with such meticulous care the illustrations appearing in this book.

To Mr. Roger Cholin for much-appreciated help.

To Technical Sergeant H. A. Johnson, Ordnance Department, for help in the selection of illustrations and captions.

J. E. H.

PREFACE

In the present crisis it has become imperative for Americans to learn of the forces that shape the outcome of battles. The factors making for either defeat or victory are many, and some of them are not entirely within the grasp of men. Yet those which depend purely on human efforts may be generally classified as morale, leadership, tactics, and ordnance. It is of the last factor, ordnance, that we wish to tell in this book. Ordnance is a general name for military supplies such as small arms, cannons, tanks, tractors, and ammunitions of all kinds. Thus our Army maintains a special service, the Ordnance Department, to provide munitions for our soldiers and to supervise the manufacture of both the defensive and offensive weapons of warfare.

Ordnance is a factor all the more important in battles, because it is upon the quality of military supplies that hinge matters of morale, leadership, and even tactics. A soldier must have complete confidence in his rifle. Weapons superior to those of the enemy enable a general to carry out his plans with a minimum of interference, and his tactics will change in accordance with the relative merits of the arms which are at his disposal. Ordnance has had a particularly important effect upon the history of Ethiopia. In 1886 the French Army adopted the Lebel rifle and rejected Daudeteau's gun. A few thousand pieces of the latter type were sold to Ras Menelik, an Ethiopian war lord. It was one of the first small caliber rifles (8mm.) fed by a magazine carrying five cartridges. When the Italians tried to conquer Ethiopia in 1897 they met defeat at Aduwa, where Ras Menelik's men sent small bullets propelled by smokeless powder to a greater distance, with much more speed and accuracy, than the Italian rifle could give with its 11-mm. caliber and its black-powder cartridges. Thus, superior ordnance rather than leadership or tactics made it possible for semicivilized peoples to repel the aggression of a well-trained European army.

A civilization's first task is self-defense, and the best of that civilization—its inventive genius, its productive power, all its resources—must strive to give the country the best tools of war. Defensive and offensive weapons must keep in step with advancing science. A modern rifle is even more a symbol of our mechanical progress than the automobile or the radio, for the last two thrive only behind the wall of security that our armed forces provide. Our Army consists not only of a group of men eager to defend their country; it includes numerous technicians, specialists in all fields of human effort, whose duty it is to keep abreast of potential enemies.

The Ordnance Department alone has a task full of responsibilities. It has been an important factor in shaping the course of our nation's history since it must select those weapons which stand by our soldiers whenever the enemy strikes. Indeed, it has played an even more important part in furthering the evolution of all arms. It is the purpose of this book to study that part, to trace the development of weapons such as the pistol, the rifle, and the cannon, so that laymen may know the problems involved in the use of our Army's more modern tools. We have centered attention upon the arms which the country has used since General Washington's time, although it has been necessary to glance over the progress made prior to the American Revolution as well as over the Continental innovations which have influenced the general trend of arms. Through this historical treatment we have attempted to explain the perennial limitations which inventors are still trying to overcome and which check the capacity of weapons. Inasmuch as tactics depend upon the weapons available, it is necessary for the citizens who would understand the problems of warfare and interpret its vicissitudes to turn a few leaves of the United States Ordnance history.

This book is in no sense an official publication or text, nor is it intended as such. It does not represent the opinions of the Ordnance Department nor of the War Department of the United States, the author alone being responsible for the book.

JAMES E. HICKS
MAJOR, ORDNANCE DEPARTMENT
ARMY OF THE UNITED STATES

August, 1941

CHAPTER ONE

PISTOLS AND REVOLVERS

THE PISTOL, perhaps more than any other weapon, affords an interest common to both the soldier and the civilian. It is primarily defensive, and self-defense is a major consideration of the soldier in times of war and of the civilian in times of peace. The pistol, like a faithful dog ready to enforce the dictates of his master, watches over the people who have trained it so that they may work and play at ease. Yet when one pictures the clumsy pistol first invented in Pistoia near Florence in 1540, when one considers its slow evolution to the neat, death-dealing weapon of today, one understands the important task performed by the Army with its continual experimentation and its wide, practical means of testing. Thus the history of the American pistol can only be written in terms of our Army's needs and of the limitations of man.

The pistol, it is true, had already passed through various stages of improvements when the United States Army came into being. Europeans had discarded the primitive matchlock type after 1635. It was a heavy, awkward weapon, ranging from a foot to a foot and a half in length. The barrel was smoothly bored and affixed to a wooden stock. The owner had to load the piece through the muzzle: he poured the powder into the barrel and

rammed the ball in with a rod. He placed a few grains
of powder in a minute pan which was an integral part
of the lock plate on the right side of the stock and which
communicated with the main charge in the barrel by
means of a touchhole or tunnel. He then pulled the
trigger, and the cock, like a curved monkey wrench holding a lighted wick clamped between its two jaws, lowered
it into the pan. The wick ignited the priming charge,
which in turn communicated with the powder in the
barrel, causing it to explode. It generally took the owner,
even the experienced owner, well over two minutes to
complete the cycle of loading and firing.

To carry a smoldering piece of cord during a campaign was not only cumbersome but also dangerous, because loose powder was always evident. The weather,
moreover, had to be clement since wind and rain could
extinguish the flame. It was essential to find a way of
producing fire when, and only when, it was needed. In
Nuremberg, Germany, around 1515, the wheel-lock system was devised. It consisted of a cock clamping between
its two jaws a piece of pyrites which, upon release of the
trigger, was lowered and touched the serrated rim of a
wheel placed at the bottom of the pan. A spring, wound
by means of a key similar to that of a toy automobile,
activated the toothed wheel which rapidly revolved and
rubbed against the pyrites. Sparks resulted which ignited
the pan charge. The lock mechanism was complicated
for the times and, being something of a work of art, was
too expensive to be widely used by common soldiers.

Flint first appeared around the beginning of the seventeenth century, and by 1695 the flintlock pistol had

superseded all other models. The cock with flint resembled the neck of a goose holding a stubby, irregular cigar in its beak. A hood called the frizzen covered the pan, over which it was held in a shut position by a spring, the frizzen spring, situated on the outside of the lock plate. When the flint hit the hinged cover (frizzen), it drove the cover forward and over, uncovering the pan and allowing the shower of sparks to fall into the pan, thereby igniting the priming charge. The pan was practically waterproof.

The flintlock pistol was in general use upon the advent of the American Revolutionary War in 1776, and it was destined to remain on the scene for the next sixty years. It was, no doubt, a clumsy weapon; a single shot was fired upon release of the trigger and it had to be loaded through the muzzle after each shot. Its caliber was .69 of an inch and the ball weighed one ounce. It was only accurate at very short ranges. Since the Army required the pistol for fighting at close quarters, it sacrificed high accuracy and long range for maneuverability. Backwoodsmen and hunters preferred their muskets and rifles, for, up to a certain extent and with other conditions being equal, the longer the barrel, the more accurate the gun.

Not only was the usefulness of a pistol confined to self-defense, but the price of an ordinary model was high because the supply was limited. Americans, with their practical turn of mind, favored the musket or rifle, better suited to the more primitive surroundings. Inasmuch as it took an experienced gunsmith some time to make one, most pistols were imported from Europe, where the industry flourished because of incessant warfare. The prominent type was the French Army's Model 1763. Only one doubled-ringed band of brass fixed the barrel to the walnut stock and the ramrod (used for loading) slipped into the stock under the barrel.

In 1775, when the revolutionary spirit was brewing, Committees of Safety were established in the various cities to procure arms and ammunition. The ingenious Americans could manufacture powder at home and could even melt ornaments of lead into balls. But, after they had contracted all the local gunsmiths, they still had to import large quantities of weapons from France. These muskets and pistols remained in the service long after peace had been made with England.

Many of the soldiers who enlisted for short terms were loath to relinquish their arms when they left the Army. Others deliberately stole them. To remedy the abuse, General Washington ordered, in 1777, that all government arms be branded with the letters "U.S." The precaution left enough weapons at the end of the war to the young nation to meet the requirements of its small peacetime army of about fifteen hundred men.

In 1794, when the thundering echoes of a European war reached our shores from across the Atlantic, when the boisterous French envoy Citizen Genêt toured the thirteen newly United States, Congress appropriated money for the establishment of two national armories in which the country might make its own muskets and pistols, thus being free from dependence on Europe to supply us with essential military requisites. The sites had to be relatively accessible, but it was also preferable to have them removed from centers of population. West Point was rejected because the Hudson River was too navigable. Springfield, Massachusetts, situated above the falls of the Connecticut River—falls that could keep foreign warships away—was selected as well as Harpers Ferry, Virginia, located on the Potomac, well above the falls. The Springfield Armory remains today our principal source of small-arms, and the Harpers Ferry Armory supplied small-arms until it was destroyed by fire in April, 1861, and never rebuilt.

Congress again appropriated money in 1798 to secure additional arms, for the danger of war with France was constantly growing. The insulting proposals made to the United States envoys in Paris by the three emissaries (X,Y,Z) of Prince Talleyrand created a tension which was eased only by the caution of President Adams. Thus, in 1799, the first government contract was made with a private gunsmith, Simeon North of Berlin, Connecticut, for five hundred pistols at the cost of six dollars each. They were based on the French Army's Model 1777, which differed from the preceding type in that the frizzen spring (the spring activating the pan cover) was reversed and a brass frame enclosed the lock action.

The first contract was not yet completed when Simeon North received a second in February, 1800, to manufacture fifteen hundred additional pistols of the same type. The two contracts were issued by James McHenry, the then secretary of war. A provision was included, as in all previous agreements, for the proof and inspection of each pistol before the government would accept its delivery. In a letter to the purveyor of public supplies in 1794, President Washington had centered attention upon the need of redressing the abuses which the government suffered at the hands of unscrupulous gunmakers. The use of bad material and faulty workmanship united to make weapons sometimes more dangerous to the operator than to the enemy. It was provided that the chief armorer should furnish an inspector to prove the arms upon the premises of the manufacturer. The inspection took place in a walled enclosure; doubly

FIGURE 1. *Model 1799, .69-cal. contract single-shot flintlock pistol. Made by Simeon North of Berlin, Conn., copied from a French Model 1777 pistol.*

loaded pistol barrels were placed on a wooden rack by series of ten or more, and the inspector ignited the charge by means of a rod so that no harm could come to him. A certain percentage of the barrels usually burst, and the government refused to accept any that were damaged. If, at a later stage in the manufacture, the inspector found the completed pistols defective in any way, the government rejected those as well, so that gunmakers were free to sell such unsatisfactory weapons to private individuals or to the masters of ships.

The National Armory at Harpers Ferry produced, in 1805, the first pistols to be made in a United States government establishment. Henry Dearborn (1751–1829), the secretary of war under Jefferson, the general who captured York and Fort George during the War of 1812, and at one time our representative in Portugal, ordered their construction. They were horsemen's pistols. The caliber was that of a rifle, namely, .54, taking a half-ounce ball. A small brass sight sat upon the barrel near the muzzle. Until that time a front sight had not been deemed necessary. The handle was so curved that, upon

FIGURE 2. *Model 1805, .54-cal. single-shot flintlock pistol. First pistol made at a national armory. (Harpers Ferry Armory, Virginia.)*

seizing the pistol and pointing it, the soldier would find that the line of his arm was merely extended. Since high accuracy at long range was not the goal, it was only essential to point the weapon toward the target.

An increase in the regiments of the Army took place in 1807. The secretary of war, therefore, instructed Tench Coxe, the purveyor of public supplies, to contract for two thousand pairs of pistols. He made the contracts with various private gunmakers, chief of which were Lancaster and York, Pennsylvania riflemakers. To ensure uniformity of design, Coxe had a Harpers Ferry pistol passed around as a pattern. Its cock or hammer

did not have the graceful curves of a gooseneck, but it
was much stronger since it was reinforced. The walnut
stock, moreover, reached nearly to the muzzle.

Through the agency of Tench Coxe, the government
made another contract with Simeon North in 1812 for a
thousand pairs of pistols. The caliber was that of the
musket, namely, .69, taking an ounce ball. The price was
$11.78 per pair and the government agreed to advance
20 per cent of the entire cost. In 1813, Marine T. Wickham improved the pistol by fixing the stock to the barrel
with a brass ring instead of the pins used precedently.
To satisfy the needs arising out of the war with England, Callender Irvine, who had become commissary
general of purchases, contracted, on April 16 of the
same year, for twenty thousand such weapons. North had
to complete the order within five years. Wickham made
the pattern pistol at the Harpers Ferry Armory. Its
weight did not exceed $3\frac{1}{2}$ pounds. Each piece cost seven
dollars and the government advanced twenty thousand
dollars.

North was so slow in delivering the pistols that the
United States inspector, Henry H. Perkin, charged him
with filling outside orders. North in reply blamed his
tardiness on the fact that many of his pistols failed to
pass the inspection and explained that he had to sell
such arms to privateers in Boston. For an additional pay-
ment of one dollar on each pistol, North agreed, in 1816,
to reduce the caliber to .54, to put a front sight on the
forward ring of the band, and to brown the barrel and
the mountings.

Many guns became rusty when they remained in the

government cellars or when they met rain and snow in a campaign. Therefore a process called "browning" was developed to prevent deterioration. The barrel and the mountings were coated with various preparations which united chemically with the metal to forestall further oxidation. The operation was simple enough so that a soldier could rebrown his own weapon. He would plug the bore and clean the exterior of the barrel by boiling it. He would then apply the browning mixture with a sponge, rest the barrel in a warm, moderately moist room for nine hours, dip it in boiling water for six minutes, clean the flaking oxide with a hard bristle brush, and coat it again, repeating the process until five or six coats had been applied.

The Ordnance Department again made a contract with North on July 1, 1819, for twenty thousand pistols at eight dollars apiece. The pattern was manufactured after an English type. It was noted for the half-cock lock patterned on the English model. Contracts were again made in 1836 and 1840 with Robert Johnson of Middletown, Connecticut, and Asa Waters of Millbury, Massachusetts.

These pistols were the last of the flintlock type which the government ordered. Every soldier had long felt the need for improvement. Flints were expensive and easy to lose and a good flint could hardly be used more than thirty times without chipping. Even the black flints which the Americans rushed from the Ticonderoga mines to Washington's camp could not ignite more than sixty shots. It was difficult, moreover, to place the initial charge in the pan during rainy or snowy weather without spoiling the powder by moistening it. The answer to these drawbacks was the percussion cap.

First used by Forsyth in 1805 and Thomas Shaw of Philadelphia in 1814, the percussion lock had much the same design as the flintlock. The pan on the side of the stock gave way to a nipple, over the small opening of which was placed the tiny percussion cap filled with a fulminating composition. The cock was a hammer whose head fell and fitted over the percussion cap. The shock caused the cap to detonate and the resulting flash was carried to the main charge through the nipple's vent. The pistol was still a muzzle-loader. Over a period of a few years many antiquated flintlocks were converted to the percussion system in any of three different ways. The first was to thread the old touchhole and screw into it a tube into which a nipple was screwed at right angles to it. In the second method the touchhole was closed; the nipple was screwed on the top of the barrel and communicated with the charge through a new inclined hole. The third system was the bolster alteration, in which a new breech was welded to the barrel.

The pattern for the percussion-lock pistol, Model 1842, was made at the Springfield Armory. It had a caliber of .54 and took a half-ounce ball. Henry Aston of Middletown, Connecticut, received a contract in 1845 for thirty thousand pieces at six dollars and a half each. In spite of all improvements such a muzzle-loader was difficult to charge and it had to be loaded after each shot. It was left to Colt to overcome these shortcomings.

Samuel Colt was born in Hartford, Connecticut, July 19, 1814, the son of Christopher and Sara Caldwell Colt.

The father's speculation plunged the family into poverty and Samuel became indentured to a Glastonbury farmer when he was only ten years old. It was there that he heard veterans of the Revolutionary War knit the tale of Tim Murphy's shooting of General Fraser at Saratoga with his double-barreled rifle and that he resolved to invent a weapon with four or even six barrels. Samuel abandoned farming to work in his father's newly acquired dye plant at Ware, Massachusetts. He was

FIGURE 3. *Model 1842, .54-cal. single-shot percussion pistol.*

about sixteen when, on August 2, 1830, his father put him on the brig *Corlo* plying between Boston and Calcutta.

One day, while he stood on deck grasping the wheel firmly, Samuel noticed how the spokes revolved and were held in place by a clutch. An idea flashed through his head. He realized that a chambered cylinder could revolve similarly in front of a fixed barrel. From then on the revolver was a fact, for he carved a wooden model while sailing back to Boston.

Samuel Colt was able by 1831 to finance the making of two revolvers. The workmanship was performed by Chase, a gunsmith of Hartford. It blew up upon firing because there was no partition between the nipples to prevent one discharge from communicating with the other. He needed capital to promote his revolver and to give it a fair trial, and, still confident, he decided to raise it by touring the United States and Canada as an ambulatory showman demonstrating the effect of laughing gas (nitrous oxide). He left the show business in 1835 to sail for London. After obtaining rights on his revolver in England, Prussia, and France, Colt returned to Washington and received his patent on February 25, 1836. He then formed a corporation which New Jersey chartered on March 5, 1836, as the "Patent Arms Manufacture Company" of Paterson.

Revolvers were made and sold on a small scale. The economic depression of Van Buren's term and the selfish attitude of office-seeking politicians prevented Colt's weapon from standing on its merits. Colt spent much time on social lobbying so that Congress might appropriate money for a test. The Army finally tested the revolver at West Point in 1837. The Commission, composed of conservative officers, declared that the arm was not suited to the Service because of its complexity. Although Colt sold fifty revolvers to the forces in Florida during the War with the Seminoles, business lagged. One hundred and thirty dollars was probably too high a price for one revolving pistol. The Paterson plant went into bankruptcy in 1841 and ceased operation in 1842.

Colt did not manufacture arms for the next five years. He developed his submarine battery and waterproof cable. An incident occurred in 1846 which set off not only the conflict with Mexico but also Colt's meteoric rise. Colonel Cross of the United States Army was killed by a Mexican patrol. A cavalry detachment sent out under Captain Thornton to rescue him was ambushed and annihilated. Captain Thornton alone succeeded in shooting his way out with a pair of Colt revolvers. General Taylor, also discovering that many Texan officers possessed such guns, dispatched Captain Samuel H. Walker of the United States Mounted Rifles to Washington to recruit another company from Walker's home state, Maryland, and to arrange for the purchase of Colt's revolvers.

FIGURE 4. *Left, Model 1847, .44-cal. Walker-Colt Dragoon, percussion revolver (six shots). Right, .44-cal. ball combustible envelope cartridge. Used in Civil War type revolvers. Circa 1850–1865.*

On January 4, 1847, Captain Walker, acting for the secretary of war, entered into a contract with Samuel Colt for one thousand of Colt's patent repeating holster pistols, caliber .44. These "revolving holster pistols" were of a new design as to size and shape, perfected by Captain Walker and Colt. The price of each, including appendages, was twenty-eight dollars. Colt then made a contract with Eli Whitney, who agreed to manufacture the revolvers at his Whitneyville Armory near New Haven, Connecticut. This was necessary as Colt did not at that time possess a factory or any means to manufacture the pistols. On July 13, 1847, the government ordered an additional thousand pieces at the same price. Colt manufactured these himself at a plant he established in Hartford, Connecticut, with the tools and machinery which Eli Whitney furnished him as agreed in their contract.

Colt's weapon had a revolving muzzle-loading cylinder in which six chambers were bored parallel to the axis. The back of the cylinder formed the breech, for it was left solid. There was a nipple for each chamber. A chamber arrived and was locked in front of the rifled barrel so as to form one continual bore when the gun was cocked, this being accomplished by means of a finger acting on a ratchet which forced the cylinder to revolve. Pulling the trigger allowed the hammer to fall on the nipple with the percussion cap, and the charge exploded. Various models of Colt's repeating pistol were bought before and during the Civil War.

The Indians' restlessness, the settling of territories not yet under the whip of law, the discovery of gold in California, and the dispute over slavery created such a demand for revolvers that Colt's factory in Hartford became one of the first large-scale production centers in the world. The division of a revolver's manufacture into steps, with one limited and unchanging task in which each worker could perfect himself, the use of regulated, impersonal, but efficient machines to perform as many operations as possible, all made for speed and greater production. Moreover, high accuracy furnished interchangeable parts so that upon the battlefield one pistol might be used to repair ten others. These were great strides in arms making and in industry in general, and when Samuel Colt died in 1862 he could boast that few Americans had accomplished more in any field.

In 1855 the Army adopted the pistol carbine. It had a caliber of .58 and was the first muzzle-loading and single-shot piece to be rifled for the United States Services. It had a detachable shoulder stock so that a horseman could use it as a pistol, although heavy, and as a carbine for short range. The pistol carbine was equipped with a special device to avoid the use of the percussion caps, which one could easily lose, the invention of a Washington dentist, who received sixty thousand dollars from the government for his system. It was known as "Dr. Maynard's tape primer." The roll of twenty-five primers, similar to a toy cap pistol, was housed in a chamber in the lock plate. Upon cocking the piece, a primer would slip over the nipple and the hammer's fall would explode it. An ingenious idea, it worked well under favorable weather conditions; moisture, however, nullified the primer. The Army discontinued the use of the tape primer in 1861.

The advent of the Civil War ushered in confusion not only among civilians but also in the Army. The Army bought large quantities of pistols and revolvers of a variety of makes, the chief types being the Colt, the Remington of Ilion, New York, and the Lefaucheux (12mm.), imported from Paris and using a metallic pinfire cartridge. Much confidence was placed in weapons of that kind. Mosby's men, the light cavalry raiders, carried two revolvers in their saddle holsters and two in their belts. Shortly after the Civil War, around 1866, metallic cartridges came into general use; they were loaded through the breech and no longer through the muzzle. Gunmakers converted many of the Colt and Remington revolvers from their percussion system to fit the new cartridges.

From 1870 to 1898 the principal revolvers were the Colt caliber .45, a single action piece which had to be

FIGURE 5. *Left, Model 1874, .45-cal. Colt metallic cartridge revolver; .44-cal. ball metallic cartridge, Martin folded head, center fire. Circa 1866–1870.*

Right, Model 1875, .45-cal. Smith & Wesson Schofield revolver (metallic cartridge); .45-cal. ball metallic cartridge, cup primer type. Circa 1868–1880; .45-cal. ball metallic reloadable brass cartridge. Circa 1882–1900.

cocked by the thumb for each shot, and the Smith & Wesson Schofield. The caliber of Colt's revolver was reduced to .38 in the Model 1892. It was particularly this type which went through the campaigns of the war with

Spain and which even saw action in the Philippines where Moros ran to the charge. The caliber proved too small, however, for the bullet penetrated the target without dealing the blunt blow needed to down a man. In the 1909 Model, therefore, the Army decided to increase the Colt's caliber to .45. A bullet of that size could stun and stop a man.

The revolver was by this time almost perfect. Yet one problem still needed attention. A way had to be

FIGURE 6. *Left, Model 1911 A-1, .45-cal. Colt automatic pistol and magazine. Right, .45-cal. ball, Model 1911. Circa 1911–1941.*

found to exploit the lost energy to load, cock, and discharge and to repeat these operations as long as the trigger was squeezed and cartridges remained in the magazine.

Although the so-called automatic pistol is a product of the twentieth century, it has ancestors as far back as 1863. Yet it was not until the Mauser appeared in 1898 that a practical arm had been found. On April 20, 1897, John Browning (1855–1926), born in Ogden, Utah, of Mormon parents, patented his automatic pistol. The Colt Firearms Company bought his patents and, in 1911, after years of experimentation, the United States Government purchased for the Army the weapon which is officially designed as "Pistol, Automatic, Caliber .45, Model 1911." It has a length of 8½ inches and weighs 2 pounds 7 ounces. The barrel is rifled and the slide bears front and rear sights. A magazine loaded with seven cartridges fits into the grip. The Model 1911 A-1 differs in that the length of the grip safety (which locks

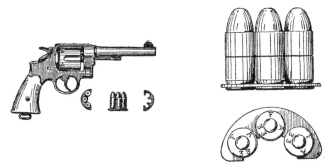

FIGURE 7. *Left, Model 1917, .45-cal. Smith & Wesson revolver. Right, .45-cal. ball, Model 1911, cartridge in cups of three for use in Model 1917 revolvers. Circa 1917–1941.*

the trigger when grasp of the handle is released) is increased and the shape of the mainspring housing (the mainspring activates the hammer) altered to fit the palm better. The only drawback is that a dud cartridge will stop all operations until it is removed from the chamber.

When the United States entered the first World War it did not have enough Model 1911 automatics to arm the vast new Army. Therefore, it bought large quantities of two commercial-type revolvers, the Colt and the Smith & Wesson. These were officially designated as:

Revolver, Colt, Caliber .45, Model 1917; Revolver, Smith & Wesson, Caliber .45, Model 1917. Both used rimmed cartridges. The United States Model 1911 used a rimless cartridge so that the Army, in order to use the standard caliber .45 United States military cartridge, had to cast about for a means by which the ejectors of the Model 1917 revolvers could grip the empty cartridge cases. It remedied the lack of rims with a flat, semicircular

FIGURE 8. *Left, Model 1918, .30-cal. automatic pistol. (Pedersen device.) Right, .30-cal. ball, Model 1918, cartridge for this pistol.*

loading clip which held three cartridges. Thus the ejectors acted on the clips and extracted the cartridge cases after the discharge of the six chambers.

Secretary of War Stimson at his press conference during the first week in August, 1941, announced that the Army is preparing to give exhaustive tests of models of two carbines, one of which will ultimately be adopted to replace virtually all caliber .45 service pistols and revolvers now in use. A full discussion of this new development will be found at the end of the rifle chapter. It seems that the carbine might supplant the revolver in the future.

CHAPTER TWO

MUSKETS

THE QUALITIES of powder and the uses to which it might be put were well known to the Chinese and also to the Moors. Yet it was not until Roger Bacon had collected the knowledge, couched it in Latin periods, and made it available to the medieval mind, not until the Hundred Years' War between England and France had revolutionized tactics and fertilized the soil for the further growth of weapons, that Europe became aware of the magic substance, powder. The beginning of the Hundred Years' War had been one of movement, with the swift thrusts of armored cavalry, of Bertrand Du Guesclin's ironclad knights raiding English strongholds. Indeed, ever since Germanic tribes had crossed Rome's frontiers, campaigns had been speedy. The German wagons had smashed Rome's infantry and the mounted nobility had trampled upon the pikemen. In 1346, however, at the famous Battle of Crécy, the English longbowmen sent shafts that pierced armors and felled horses at a long distance, and the flower of French nobility remained on the field. The longbow had reestablished the supremacy of the infantry with its pikemen.

The bow and pike remained the principal infantry weapons for the next three hundred years. The Battle of Crécy had ushered in the use of powder by means of the cannon. The need was at once felt for a cannon small enough so that one man could carry and operate it. This hand weapon had already appeared when Joan of Arc rescued the city of Orléans from the English in 1429. It consisted of a diminutive cannon or tube $1\frac{1}{2}$ feet in length fastened to a stick from 3 to 4 feet long. The gunner poured a copious charge of powder through the muzzle into the tube, followed it with a stone as round and fitting as possible, placed the stick under his left arm, not quite horizontally so that the stone would not roll out of the barrel, and thrust a red-hot wire through a vent at the base of the tube to ignite the powder. Having to carry stones, powder, and a fire to heat his ignition wire in addition to what was already a heavy weapon, the gunner could not very well run about the battlefield in the fashion of bowmen. Moreover, his piece made more din and smoke than actual killing. The handgun was, therefore, an auxiliary weapon: it fired from protected positions, playing much the same role as light artillery, trench mortars, or machine guns do today. Gunners were comparatively few; they acted as sentinels or outposts to warn of enemy approach by firing their noisy tool, and they were also stationed at the flanks to protect the troops from a flanking movement of enemy cavalry by frightening the horses. Such was the earliest ancestor of the musket.

The bore of this primitive gun was quite large, for it had to shoot a stone heavy enough to cause damage. Since the density of stone is relatively low, the missile had to be large to have sufficient weight and momentum.

As a result, the operator must have felt vigorous recoil effects. Around 1500, in order to facilitate the firing of a gun and to control the recoil action, the butt end of the stock was shortened and broadened so that the gunner could place it on his breast or thigh, thereby allowing his entire body to absorb the shock. When a soldier was about to thrust the hot wire into the vent to ignite the charge, the powder was hemmed in on one side by the breech, then by the walls of the barrel, and finally by the bullet. Upon ignition, the charge began to burn violently, quickly producing gases so voluminous that they became highly compressed and sought to escape from their prison. As they pushed the projectile in front of them out through the muzzle on their way to freedom, they struck the walls of the barrel and the breech, giving a strong backward thrust to the piece— an action known as recoil. The action was all the more disagreeable because it increased in strength as the charge of powder and the bullet became larger and heavier. Naturally the lighter the gun used, the less capable it was of withstanding the shock, which was then transferred to the gunner. His aim was spoiled, his body bruised. Indeed, the bruise was so extensive and painful that a soldier grew to expect the gun's blow after a few shots and shrank back in anticipation of the impact. This instinctive reaction became known as "flinching," and our modern infantryman still has to combat it, though to a much less degree with the modern Garand rifle.

It was at this point, early in the sixteenth century, that an unknown inventor made a time-transcending discovery. He found that if the stock was bent and placed against the body, the recoil action would first push the stock, which would then try to level up by thrusting the forward part of the gun upward. Even though the thrust was slight it absorbed part of the recoil effect, with the result that the gunner felt less of a shock. The stock was then lengthened to permit firing from the shoulder and, consequently, sighting. The gun was known as the "harquebus" after the French *arquebuse,* which in turn was an adaptation of the Italian *archibuso* (most likely from the Dutch *haakbus,* meaning a hooked butt or a gun with a hook or a bent stock). The harquebus was a handy, maneuverable weapon, for it had a length of only 3 feet and a weight of 10 pounds. Its bore was ¾ of an inch wide. It was of the matchlock type, a muzzle-loader, and could fire one lead bullet— lead had replaced stone because of its density and comparative abundance—every two minutes. It was not effective above 100 yards and the numerous misfires caused by powder impurities clogging the touchhole from the priming pan to the chamber limited its services to those of an auxiliary weapon.

Powder was indeed a capricious substance. Among other things Bacon had told the world two important facts: that powder was composed of saltpeter, charcoal, and sulphur and that the mixture should be wetted. Men had heeded the first part and forgotten the second. The mixture was made before the beginning of a campaign and carried over bad roads on the way to the battlefield; upon being shaken, the ingredients separated into different layers according to their respective weights, thus making the substance practically useless. Gunners, and especially cannoneers, later on took the habit of carrying the ingredients in separate casks and of concocting their mixtures upon the battlefield. The excitement of an engagement was not conducive to fine, uniformly mixed products, so that no two charges were alike. Also added to this difficulty was the matter of packing the powder into the barrel. If it was pressed too tightly, the igniting fire could not penetrate the charge and only part of the powder could explode, expelling the rest with the bullet. Sometimes the charge did not explode at all and this, along with the task of mixing powder upon the battlefield, made the job of gunners and cannoneers a very hazardous one.

During the early part of the sixteenth century, somewhere around 1530, men remembered Bacon's second advice and began to wet their powder. The powder maker thoroughly mixed the saltpeter, the sulphur, and the charcoal. He watered the dustlike matter, washing away all the impurities that could not burn and which befouled the touchhole and the barrel. He then allowed the powder to dry and to cake. He broke it into flakes, an operation which gave the product the name of "corned powder." Such a granulated charge exposed more surface to combustion. It was therefore easier to ignite and it burned much more violently. The explosion was so fierce that the use of powder was at first forbidden for cannons since iron's resistance to a shock does not increase in proportion with its thickness. Powder was later compressed and hardened into uniform grains, very much like the ball bearings of a toy bicycle's axle, to ensure similarity in charge and to lessen rapidity of combustion. The grains were also polished to nullify the effects of moisture. This "black powder" was to rule over battlefields for over three hundred years, and it wrought immediate changes in weapons.

The light harquebus could not withstand the violent explosion any more than could the cannon. Most barrels burst. The effect of recoil upon the soldier, moreover, increasing as the gun lightened, was so strong that one could not fire the piece without the butt's bruising the shoulder, slapping one's face, or jumping out of control. Thus, about 1540, the Spaniards introduced a gun 6 or 7 feet long, weighing from 40 to 50 pounds. It was so bulky a muzzle-loading and matchlock instrument that two men were necessary to operate it, firing with the aid of a forked stick 4 feet long planted in the ground with the fork skyward to support the heavy barrel. It took at least two minutes to load and fire the piece, and it certainly was not accurate. It was still an auxiliary weapon which fulfilled the same requirements as the machine gun or the light artillery of today, for its power was tremendous and its effective range two hundred yards.

Such was the first "musket" (from the Italian *moschetto,* meaning a hawk). Since its greatest drawback was its bulkiness, its height was subsequently reduced to 5 feet and its weight to approximately 10 pounds, thus allowing one man to operate it. Another fault, which took almost three hundred years in the solving, was the curse of misfires. The priming pan communicated with the chamber by means of a touchhole narrow enough to minimize the amount of gas escaping from the chamber and not contributing to the force that propelled the bullet. When the pan was filled with powder a little always slipped into the touchhole, which became clogged with powder ashes. The clogging prevented the ignition from getting to the main charge, and misfires resulted. Partly to overcome this difficulty, the matchlock system gave way to the wheel lock, then to the flintlock, which finally left the ground to the percussion system in 1830. Percussion caps were the most satisfactory answer to the touchhole problem.

The musket, however, was still an auxiliary weapon. Its rate of fire was slow and it took a formation five ranks in depth to secure a continuous line of fire, one rank firing while the others completed the subsequent steps in loading. And, what was still more important, a general had to depend upon pikemen for hand-to-hand fighting. It was not until 1640, in the city of Bayonne in southern France, that this last question was solved. The invention consisted of a simple knife, the base of which formed a round shank stuck in the muzzle of the barrel. It was called the "bayonet." A soldier could be either a gunner or a pikeman, for the musket could play the role of a pike although it could not fire while the bayonet was fastened. To remedy the defect, the shank was hollowed so that the soldier became both a gunner and a pikeman. Of course, the gun drove out the pike and it became the standard infantry weapon.

The increasing use of the musket as well as that of the pistol and of the rifle brought an equally increasing demand for powder. Powder, however, was not to be had so readily. One ingredient, saltpeter, was all important, and Europe was a continent particularly poor in saltpeter. Since the kings engaged in continuous warfare and since saltpeter was hard to procure, every nation kept a body of men whose sole duty was to look for sources of saltpeter and to salvage every bit found. The favorite method of obtaining the decayed vegetable matter was to tear down the stone walls of stables. As the demand increased, Europe developed a method to aid the natural process. It became known as "niter farming." Layers of mingled manure and earth were buried in darkness and warmth, two factors favoring the growth of niter-producing bacteria. To ensure a continuous supply of air, the beds were frequently stirred. When the process of nitrification was deemed sufficient, wood ashes were added to furnish the potassium necessary to displace the hydrogen in the nitric acid, thus forming potassium nitrate or saltpeter. To remove the potassium nitrate from the manure, earth, and ashes, the whole mixture was allowed to soak in water, which dissolved the saltpeter. The solution was then made to stand, and the water evaporated, leaving behind crystals of saltpeter which were ground to manufacture powder.

Niter farming was a tedious process which men continued only because of the ever-growing desire for powder. Saltpeter was so expensive that powder manufacturers were inclined to reduce the saltpeter ratio to the barest minimum, thereby increasing the percentages of sulphur and charcoal to such limits that the products furnished more noise, smoke, and ashes than propelling force. It was not until 1850 that the price of potassium nitrate fell sufficiently low to induce manufacturers to become more ethical and to allow the proper saltpeter ratio, for it was about that time that someone discovered extensive sources of sodium nitrate ($NaNO_3$) in Chile. Of course, it was a supply of sodium nitrate and not of saltpeter (KNO_3) that was obtained, and it had to be treated chemically with German earth impregnated with potassium chloride (KCl) so that the potassium of the latter might unite with the nitrate of the former to give us the potassium nitrate needed to manufacture powder. Naturally toward the very end of the nineteenth century the development of smokeless powder, which replaced black powder as a propelling agent, and the establishment of nitro-fixing plants enabled the United States as well as most other nations to become more independent of the Chilean deposits.

The colonization of North America, the dangers inherent in Indian hostility, the French and Indian War, and especially our Revolutionary War transplanted European weapons to a younger and, as the history of firearms tends to show, perhaps a richer soil. Of course, not until the beginning of the Civil War or, to be more exact, not until Colt's revolutionary ideas had ripened into deeds around 1840 did the pistol find a secure footing in America. Its short range, its comparative inaccuracy, and its uselessness in the tasks, important to the earlier Americans, of food getting made it the arm of the rich rather than that of the poor, of the officer rather than the soldier. The surroundings of a country that was still in the making did not foster the growth of the pistol. Especially during the years preceding the Declaration of Independence the few gunsmiths established upon American soil eked out a poor livelihood by satisfying the only demand which existed—that for muskets and rifles. The few pistols of American make and those imported from Europe were of such a price that only relatively few could afford them. So, in 1776, when a whole people answered the call of freedom, the musket ruled sovereign among weapons.

The Continental Congress tackled a difficult job when it attempted to supply the thousands of citizen-soldiers who swelled the ranks of the extemporaneous Army with muskets. The larger cities, of course, had on hand small stores of muskets which the governors and the colonial assemblies had bought and maintained as a precaution in case of war. That such stores were small was partly because of the Americans' reluctance to part with any money that might increase the strength and efficiency of an army which they detested for being a symbol of English control, and also because the successful conclusion of the French and Indian War had removed, to a certain extent, the dangers of war and, therefore, the need for strong militia forces. The muskets naturally were chiefly of English manufacture since the English Parliament insisted upon furnishing all the finished products which the Americans needed in exchange for raw materials. Perhaps all was for the best: few gunsmiths had yet settled in America and the English government could hardly allow any of its possessions to purchase arms from European countries.

Whatever the reasons may have been, the stores of muskets were small and armed only a fraction of the

Revolutionary Army. The Continental Congress had to find other sources of arms, and it decided to requisition all serviceable private weapons. The entire country was combed as with a rake in search of guns. Many of the dispossessed complained sincerely, for a shotgun was to most settlers as priceless a commodity as a wife: it was the magic wand that procured food and stood off the Indians' savage onslaught; it was the cherished protector that, from its position over the fireplace, looked over the hearth.

The indefinite number of muskets collected, however, could not carry us through the war. The workmanship was so poor, the models so varied, that should a part of the weapon such as a spring snap on the battlefield it was well-nigh impossible to find any part to replace it, and the musket was cast aside. As it has been already pointed out in the chapter on pistols, General Washington was singularly troubled by "the scandalous loss, waste, and private appropriation of public arms . . ." During the six ominous months following the American withdrawal from Long Island a major portion of those muskets vanished, and the English accentuated the disaster by capturing thousands of firelocks at Fort Washington. Indeed, had Howe pressed his advantage as the winter drew to an end in 1777 he would have met an army equipped with one musket—and a bad one at that—for every two men.

Meanwhile the colonies with their assemblies and the large cities with their Committees of Safety tried to outdo one another in procuring muskets. They employed all local gunsmiths, issuing contracts for complete muskets, seldom for more than one hundred at a time, or for parts that could be assembled with what was imported. The gunsmiths were not many, however; their capacity was insignificant. Commercial European makers shipped some of their products, but they evidently took too much advantage of the Americans' plight, furnishing despicable arms at an exorbitant price, for agencies had to discontinue such purchases.

The question of procuring muskets was so pressing and hopeless that Benjamin Franklin, who was on the Philadelphia Committee of Safety at the beginning of the Revolutionary War, wrote to Charles Lee, at the time fortifying the port of New York, expressing the belief that the musket might well be discarded.

"But I still wish that the pike could be introduced, and I would add bows and arrows. These were good weapons not lightly cast aside: 1) Because a man may shoot as truly with a bow as with a common musket; 2) He can discharge four arrows in the time of charging and discharging one bullet; 3) His object is not taken from his view by the smoke on his own side; 4) A flight of arrows, seen coming upon them, terrifies and disturbs the enemies' attention to their business; 5) An arrow striking in any part of a man puts him hors-du-combat till it is extracted; 6) Bows and arrows are more easily provided than muskets and ammunition."

In spite of Franklin's seemingly good sense, he probably had bent that sense to serve practicability rather than truth, for the wars in Europe and the very conquest of America had given ample evidence of the musket's superiority. A bullet carries more force and confusion than an arrow, and it does so by remaining invisible in its flight whereas an arrow can easily be dodged.

Matters suddenly took a turn for the better. Largely through the influence of Benjamin Franklin, who was loved and admired in France because of his work as scientist and philosopher, Silas Deane, our worldly envoy to Louis XVI, succeeded in gaining the confidence of Beaumarchais. Beaumarchais (1732–1799), who attained a prominent place in French literature with his two plays *Le Barbier de Séville* and *Le Mariage de Figaro,* was a witty and elegant courtier at Versailles. He sojourned some time in England where he gained a sincere admiration for the American Revolution. He determined to help the thirteen colonies to his utmost, not solely because they were fighting for freedom but also because they might weaken hostile England.

Beaumarchais convinced Louis XVI's ministers that France should arm the struggling colonies. As a result, Penet, the chief armorer at the Royal Arsenal at Charleville, was allowed to sell some thirty thousand muskets of the French Army Model 1763 at twenty-three francs each to armorers in various French cities. The armorers then transferred the weapons to American authorities, and three merchantmen loaded with the whole consignment soon left the French coast. One of these fell prey to the British Navy's blockade, but by March, 1777, a vessel carrying eleven thousand muskets sailed up the Delaware River to Philadelphia, while another alighted in Portsmouth, New Hampshire, to unload twelve thousand guns. The problem of supplying Washington's Army with muskets was solved, for about eighty thou-

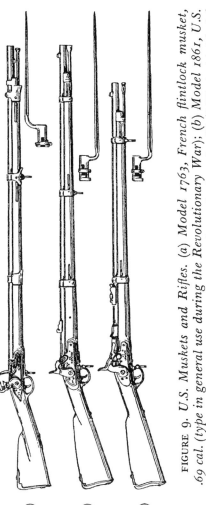

FIGURE 9. *U.S. Muskets and Rifles.* (a) *Model 1763, French flintlock musket, .69 cal. (type in general use during the Revolutionary War); (b) Model 1861, U.S. percussion musket, .58 cal. (type in general use during the Civil War); (c) Model 1873, U.S. breech-loading rifle, .45 cal. (Springfield) (type used in Indian Wars).*

sand stands of arms arrived here in the course of the war.

A large part of those muskets were of the French Army Model 1763. It was a flintlock, single-shot piece with a smoothly bored barrel having a caliber of .69. The iron pan had a fence to prevent the powder from escaping; the frizzen had a curl at the foot and at the upper back. The hammer was reinforced and the head of the screw used to tighten the two flint-holding hammer jaws was pierced to facilitate turning it. Three bands, retained by a spring looking to the rear, held the barrel to the walnut stock. The forward band had an upper and a lower ring, with a brass sight squat on the latter one. The middle band, as well as the trigger guard, had an oval sling swivel. Two screws held the butt plate to the stock. The ramrod, used in pushing the bullet down the barrel, was of iron, with the exception of a pear-shaped head which was of steel. The total length of the musket was 5 feet and the bayonet raised that total to 6 feet.

It is surprising that France depleted to such an extent her stocks of a model that was comparatively recent. It was not because of financial needs, since France had to lend money to the thirteen states to enable them to buy the guns. It was rather hostility for England and perhaps the rearmament of French forces with the Model 1777 which made the previous type obsolete. Among the eighty thousand guns imported there were also earlier models of regulation military muskets. Enough of these muskets remained after peace with England had been signed to arm the small peacetime American Army.

It was not until 1794, when diplomatic relations with

France became strained, that Congress appropriated
money not only for the establishment of the two national armories but also for the purchase of additional
arms. Inasmuch as there was no domestic supply of muskets the government had to look abroad. The United
States minister to London, during the years 1794 and
1795, received in exchange over one hundred thousand
dollars with which to secure cannons and arms. Ship
after ship sailed into the Delaware River up to Philadelphia, some from London, others from Hamburg,
loaded with scores of cannons, thousands of flints, and
numerous casks packed with twenty muskets each. The
purveyor of public supplies received all told about seven
thousand muskets costing nine dollars apiece. This was
the last large import of arms from abroad; thereafter
the Springfield and Harpers Ferry Armories, along with
a host of private gunsmiths located chiefly in the New
England and Atlantic states, would satisfy the nation's
need for weapons.

The Springfield Armory, which was located in buildings previously belonging to the United States Government, was the first public institution to turn out muskets in America, although the number for the year 1795
did not exceed 245. They were patterned after the
French Model 1763 and the lock plates bore the letters
"U.S.," an eagle, and the word "Springfield." One must
not be surprised if the Army did not choose the French
Model 1777 as a pattern, for France was not friendly at
the time and it was probably impossible to buy enough
specimens to serve as patterns. Secretary of War Mc-
Henry (1796–1800) ordered that a bayonet be perma-

nently soldered on the barrel of each musket. Fifteen thousand such weapons were completed when Secretary of War Henry Dearborn discontinued the practice in 1806. He also ordered that the barrels be shortened by 12 inches so that the short musket stood approximately 4 feet. Later on this was considered such a waste that the government sold fifteen thousand muskets to William Cramond of Philadelphia, who supplied filibusters operating in the Caribbean Sea.

In 1798, Secretary of the Treasury Oliver Wolcott issued the first contracts made with private gunsmiths to manufacture muskets. Twenty-seven contractors were alloted a total of 40,200 guns at the price of $13.40 each. Eli Whitney of New Haven, Connecticut, famous as the "cotton gin inventor," was to make ten thousand. In 1801, Whitney saw a French Army Model 1777; he was impressed and proposed to make improvements on the remaining part of his contract, a suggestion which the government approved. Most other contracts were for guns five hundred to two thousand in number. The French Model 1763 or the Springfield Armory Model 1795 served as patterns. The contracts specified that all guns "should be finished in a workmanlike manner, in all parts precisely or as near as possible, conformably to two patterns"; that "the stocks of the muskets should be made of well-seasoned black walnut timber, when the same could be procured by the contractor, otherwise, of well-seasoned, tough maple timber." The gunmakers, however, had had no previous experience and they did not make deliveries before some years. Their products, moreover, were of such poor workmanship that many of their muskets could not pass the government inspection. As a matter of fact, Colonel Whiting, who commanded the Fourth Infantry, proposed that the arms be sold for shipment to Africa or South America.

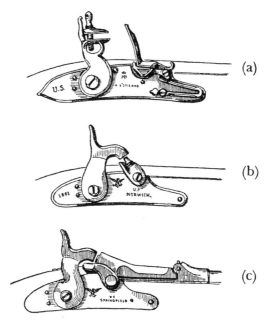

FIGURE 10. *Actions of U.S. Muskets and Rifles.* (a) *Model 1763, French flintlock musket, .69 cal.;* (b) *Model 1861, U.S. percussion musket, .58 cal.;* (c) *Model 1873, U.S. breech-loading rifle, .45 cal. (Springfield).*

On April 28, 1808, Congress passed an act appropriating two hundred thousand dollars annually for "arming and equipping the whole body of Militia." Newspapers in the larger cities carried advertisements asking interested parties to bid for contracts to manufacture muskets. According to a report of Tench Coxe, the purveyor of public supplies, in 1810, eighteen firms obtained contracts to make a total of eighty-two thousand weapons based upon patterns resembling the French Model 1763, while the government advanced $88,343.50. Anticipating slow deliveries and poor workmanship, Tench Coxe forwarded a strong warning to each contractor. The exhortation was of no avail.

The government should have learned by that time that it could not rely upon private factories to supply the vital war needs of ordnance. Yet when the War of 1812 broke out the secretary of state resorted to the same device. Marine T. Wickham, who was then employed at the Philadelphia Laboratory, designed a new model in 1812. The only important innovation was fixing the bayonet to the barrel by means of a screw, and even this change was not made in the contracts that followed. Wickham went to Harpers Ferry to supervise the manufacture of the patterns. Eli Whitney, among others, was asked to manufacture fifteen thousand guns at seventeen dollars each. He submitted such a different musket that Callender Irvine wished to terminate the contract. The episode ended with this letter which Irvine wrote to Secretary of War Armstrong:

"We cannot rely on contractors for a supply of arms. Those private contracts are exceptionable in many respects, nay in every respect. Better to increase the number of our establishments and the number of hands at those in operation and bring the whole under the superintendence of one judicious and independent man. It will be safer for the government to expend two or three thousand dollars on building Armouries than to advance so much money to individuals who will expend it on erecting buildings and machinery for themselves and disappoint the Government, as to a supply of arms confidentially calculated to be received within the period specified in their contracts."

The wise words fell on barren soil. In 1816, Colonel Wadsworth of the Ordnance Department ordered that pattern muskets with a lock similar to that of the French Army Model 1777 be made at the Harpers Ferry Armory. Because of insistence on the uniformity of patterns, because some patterns were misplaced in New York, because extensive experiments on browning were conducted under the direction of Lieutenant Colonel Bomford, it was not before 1821 that uniform patterns were ready to serve as guides for both public and private armories. Following the lead of the British Army, the barrels were browned. The brass pan was inclined, the frizzen bent back, the frizzen spring turned down, and the comb of the stock straight. In spite of all this trouble to establish uniform patterns, private arms makers continued to furnish weapons of inferior quality.

In an effort to put an end to the confusion which the variety of Army weapons caused and to centralize the buying organization, a board of officers convened in Washington late in 1831. Its job "was to establish a uniform system in the operations of the Ordnance Department." The board appointed a committee of two, Colonels Eustis and Bomford, to conduct experiments and research as to what European powers did in order to report to the board a proper caliber and model for muskets. The committee selected the French Model 1822, and the pattern muskets subsequently made at Harpers Ferry Armory were marked Model 1835 on the barrel. Because the Army was small, the officers who had been on ordnance duty were so busy with the Seminole War that it was not before late 1838 that armories were or-

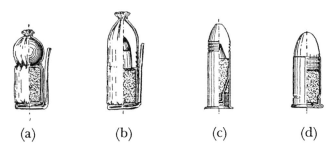

(a)   (b)   (c)   (d)

FIGURE 11. *Small-arms cartridges. (a) Round ball paper cartridge. Circa 1600–1865; (b) elongated ball paper cartridge (Minié type). Circa 1855–1865; (c) metallic cartridge, center fire, Morse type, 1857; (d) metallic cartridge, rim fire. Circa 1865.*

dered to commence tooling up for the new model. A few minor alterations in 1840 postponed production still further.

It was a flintlock musket, with a smoothly bored barrel of caliber .69. The gun had a total length of 58 inches. The finger ridges on the guard plate of the original French model were discarded. Even more important, however, was the fact that the parts of the lock mechanism, such as the tumbler and the sear, which suffer wear because of the friction caused by each squeeze of the trigger, were made of steel to ensure greater resistance. The Springfield Armory manufactured the muskets until 1844; private contractors, until 1848. It was the last flintlock model used by the Services. The percussion-lock system superseded it.

It has already been brought out in the chapter on pistols that flintlocks were expensive and not practical in rainy weather. That they should have given way to the percussion locks is not as surprising as the fact that they did so only twenty-five years after discovery. Naturally the Army was conservative and careful lest it should invest money in a worthless experiment.

In 1841 work at the two national armories began on percussion arms for the Service. The Model 1841 rifle and Model 1842 musket and pistol resulted; this musket was the first percussion and the last smoothbore. This was the last development of the musket proper. The smoothbore barrel had gone through all the improvements it was to receive. Breechloaders, metallic cartridges, and automatic systems were to fare better with the rifled barrel. So, in 1855, the muskets were rifled and a new arm appeared under the name of rifle-musket. Although the new weapon was really a compromise between the musket and the rifle, or rather a marriage of the two, blending the advantages of both, it took only twenty years for the rifle with its potentialities to stamp out all vestiges of the musket as an infantry weapon.

CHAPTER THREE

RIFLES

A RIFLE is a shoulder weapon, the barrel of which has its interior grooved with cutin lines parallel to one another and revolving so that, should a grain of powder slide bobsledlike down a groove from the breech to the muzzle, it would turn around the inside of the barrel, the number of turns varying with different types of rifles. Why should the small matter of barrel rifling mother such an important class of shoulder weapons? The answer lies in the fact that the grooves change the whole manner in which a projectile travels on to its goal. Should the reader ever wander over a battlefield and pick up a stray bullet from a rifle or a machine gun, he would notice at once the twisting linear indentations that corset the missile. He would notice also that the grooves are parallel and that, were they continued on an imaginary line, they would complete one turn in about 10 inches, whereas one hundred years ago they would have completed one turn in 6 feet.

In order to know the cause of those indentations, one must understand what happens to a bullet when a cartridge is fired. First, whether it is loaded through the breech or the muzzle, the bullet must fit as snugly and tightly over the powder into the barrel as possible. When the powder is ignited and explodes, a chemical reaction, a form of oxidation takes place which produces large quantities of gases. The gases further expand in volume because of the considerable heat which the combustion generates. The bolt's solid fit into the breech and the metallic cartridge case's tight seal form a wall on one side, while on the other the snug bullet offers temporary resistance and prevents gas leakage. The expanding gases are imprisoned and compressed until they force the side offering less resistance to give way. Of course, it is the bullet that must concede and move into the barrel, and the gases' pressure upon its base is so great that it becomes deformed and is compelled to take the shape of the rifled tube. The softer lead bullet or its cupronickel jacket fills the bore's grooves, and it is forced to rotate in the same direction and speed of twist as those of the grooves. As it leaves the muzzle the missile continues to spin on its own axis, completing so many turns to the minute.

The importance of the spinning action is great. The reader has at one time or another thrown stones. If he has ever chosen two small, flat, circular pebbles, sent one through the air by sheer force and caused the other to rotate on its own axis, he must of necessity have found that the latter cleaved space regularly and completed a longer run more directly. Better still, he has surely tossed around a football. Upon throwing it naturally, the reader must have seen his toy tumbling over itself, executing turns, and wasting energy in somersaults as air resistance increased its deviation from the true mark. Its line of flight resembled an accentuated but irregular curve. He soon learned to throw it by pointing it toward the target and causing it to spin upon its own axis.

Such a pass, with the ball rotating, was more direct, that is, its line of flight was more parallel to the earth; it did not deviate as much from the intended course and it flew more speedily. In order to understand the cause of the improvement we must realize that once a ball is on its own there are three forces which influence its voyage. The first, and indubitably the most important, is the gravitational pull that draws all bodies to the earth. The second is the resistance which the atmosphere offers. It varies with the temperature and moisture. A bullet or a ball will travel faster through dry air, where it need not displace water molecules in the gaseous state. It will fly faster when the weather is warm, when it can easily displace molecules of air which high temperature already puts in constant motion. There are also atmospheric agents such as rain, snow, and wind which check or alter the course of a bullet or football. The third force, pitted against the other two in a struggle which it always loses, is the speed of the projectile as it leaves the muzzle. This muzzle velocity naturally depends on the strength of the propelling agent (either the powder charge or the arm muscle in case of a ball), and it is either sustained by a proper spin or reduced by the lack of a spin or by an improper one. Atmospheric resistance is the first force that tends to check the speed of a missile, and not until it has fairly succeeded does the gravitation effect work its havoc.

A bullet suffers from shortcomings similar to those of a football. The cylindrical projectile spinning through the air flies a flatter trajectory, races on toward the target more accurately and swiftly, and obtains a longer range than would a musket's leaden ball, for the latter must needs form an arc having as extremities the muzzle on the one hand and, on the other, the distant point where the law of gravity calls home to earth the erratic lead. A modern rifle's missile travels on a line almost parallel to the ground, thus allowing the operator to sight his gun carefully. The energy saved by eliminating the gain in height is used to increase the bullet's range. Besides, a spinning object offers less surface to the interference of wind and rain, and it is thereby steadied in its course.

It is evident that a rifle is superior to a musket. Yet that superiority depends chiefly upon two requisites: the bolt must fit into the breech so as to form, along with the cartridge case's base, a solid, gastight wall, and the bullet must stopple the barrel so as to make another wall, though of less resistance. The two problems are connected. If a rifle is a muzzle-loader, the breech will naturally be solid and offer no trouble. The difficulty comes when a bullet large enough to prevent gas leakage has to be hammered into the barrel. The bullet is never large enough to fit the grooves well and the hammering in damages the ball. On the other hand, if the rifle is a breechloader, a satisfactory bullet goes into the chamber, thus establishing one wall. The gist of the matter is to make that the wall of least resistance. In other words, a way must be found to close the breech solidly so that no gas leakage will result. The only solution was the use of the metallic cartridge case.

In spite of the complexities entailed in rifling, one

must not assume that it is a recent invention. If we have described some of the principles involved by using a modern rifle as a manikin, so to speak, we did it with a view to fostering a grasp of the general problems check-ing the use of rifling for over three centuries and of the developments that caused its hectic rise. The ancient Greek discobolus knew that he had to impart a rotating motion to his discus if he wanted to gain a good distance. Even primitive people realized that spinning steadied a projectile in its flight. Yet it was not until the early days of the sixteenth century that an unknown inventor, most likely belonging to the Nuremberg school of armorers, applied the common knowledge to firearms by boring spiral grooves within the barrel. In order to spin the ball the grooves had to grip it tightly so that a projectile slightly larger than the barrel's diameter was rammed down through the muzzle. What was already a difficult loading operation became much more strenuous and nearly impossible when the ashes of previous powder charges befouled the grooves and the barrel.

It was only natural that the rifle's earlier missiles should have been of a spherical type similar to that of the musket. The loose ball of a musket, however, bounced up and down within the barrel, the last im-pact influencing the ball's trajectory, which could be low, high, or sideways according to what part of the barrel the ball hit last when leaving the muzzle. This defect was somewhat remedied by fitting the bullet tightly to the smoothbore. It was recognized early that an elongated, cylindrical bullet would not have this disadvantage but would possess a more evil fault. Upon flight, and since the bullet's weight was not equally distributed, the heavier base, receiving the major share of the propelling force and having the more momentum, would tend to assume the lead, for air resistance has more effect upon a light than a heavy object if the surface is the same. Thus the elongated bullet would always topple over. Of course, spinning nullified that fault by its tendency to keep the point forward. Such a bullet, however, would have been much harder to ram down a rifled barrel because of the increased surface which the grooves had to grip. Thus the ball, with merely its circumference contacting the rifling, was retained for the rifle as well as for the musket until a more satisfactory method of loading could be found.

The curse of muzzle-loading practically prohibited the extensive use of the rifle. Christian IV, king of Denmark, attempted around 1600 to arm some of his troops with wheel-lock rifles but failed. In the seventeenth century Marshal Puységur recommended that two men in each company be armed with a rifle, and by 1660 some French cavalry carried a rifled weapon. Nevertheless, the difficulty of loading restricted the use of the new arm. A few attempts were made to limit the time necessary to complete the operation. Gustavus Adolphus, for instance, issued the first cartridge, a paper envelope comprising black powder and ball, so that his soldiers would not waste time measuring powder. Frederick the Great himself, in 1750, tried to increase his soldiers' rate of fire by supplying them with an iron ramrod and by dividing the loading operation into a number of mechanical steps. His success was limited.

Another problem confused early riflemakers. They had to determine which type of groove would best cause a ball to rotate. A shallow spiral line cut into the barrel was most favored. Its only defect lay in that it quickly became clogged with powder ashes, particularly adhesive because of the high carbon content. The turns of the rifling, moreover, could not be too steep; otherwise the bullet would have raced through the bore without following the grooves. In 1725 a Spaniard invented a type known later on as the "Brunswick." Two deep grooves, into which a spherical bullet belted in the middle with a ridge could fit easily, were bored within the barrel opposite one another. Having an unbalanced form, the bullet flew badly and did not meet air resistance equally on all parts. It was therefore not adopted. The loading difficulties soon discouraged the Europeans, and their armies abandoned the rifle to those who, like hunters and pioneers, needed accuracy rather than speedy operation.

The American pioneers quickly recognized the value of a weapon which could hit a deer at 200 yards, twice the range of a musket. So trappers and frontiersmen kept their rifles and their prowess during the French and Indian War induced the English to establish a Royal American Regiment armed with the gun. British officers also carried rifles, and Wolfe, who died in 1759, possessed one of American make. Americans owed not a little of their skill in its use to a new method of loading which they had devised as early as 1700. It was known as "patch-loading."

The gunner first poured the powder into the barrel;

he placed a patch or square piece of linen over the muzzle, set the ball over the orifice, and rammed the whole thing down. The linen pressed into the grooves prevented gas leakage by fitting the chamber tightly, the patched bullet stored greater gas pressure before departing, and the increased pressure gave a higher velocity to the ball. Inasmuch as the pressure augmented, the recoil also became greater. The gun kicked so hard that it often spoiled the aim and bruised the shoulder, and in order to reduce the kick the operator was led to put a smaller charge of powder, thus limiting the pressure, the speed of the ball, and its range. To settle the difficulty riflemakers lowered the caliber from .69 taking a one-ounce ball (caliber of the musket) to .54 taking a half-ounce missile. With the same charge the smaller ball, meeting less air resistance, traveled at a greater speed and retained the hitting power of the larger projectile. Although the loading was slow, the American pioneers were well pleased with the other advantages and the rifle really became an American weapon during the eighteenth century.

The British found that from the outset of the American Revolutionary War General Washington had armed some soldiers with rifles in every company, where their duty was to act as sharpshooters, picking off enemy officers at long distance. The British met the menace by pitting rifle against rifle. They even introduced a breech-loading rifle. Men had realized at an early period the advantages of breech-loading, for, added to the slowness of muzzle-loading, there was the constant danger of a spark from the preceding shot lingering in the barrel

and igniting the powder charge poured down for reloading. To avoid accidents in muzzle-loading, operators
usually took the habit of sponging the bore with a damp
swab between each shot. Cavalrymen naturally could not
charge a muzzle-loader while riding. The need for an
efficient breechloader was urgent. One system of breech-
loading which was adopted for cannons consisted of a
separate breech piece wedged in place in the rear of the
main tube after charging. Another method was to use
a breech plug which closed and opened the bore by
screwing in and out like a bolt. Of course, one of the
earliest ideas, which is still applied to shotguns, was to
open the bore by dropping the hinged barrel. The important thing was to arrive at a device capable of preventing disastrous gas leakage—gas leakage which dimin-
ished the power behind a bullet, which might scorch the
firer's face and hands, and which might clog the lock
mechanism. The device, moreover, had to work quickly
and simply so as to continue functioning even though
the heat of firing expanded the chamber.

The British breechloader met nearly all the requirements rather well, considering the times. The inventor,
Lieutenant Colonel Patrick Fergusson of the 71st High-
landers, made his weapon in England and successfully
demonstrated it at Woolwich in 1776. The breech
opened and closed by means of a vertical plug threaded
with a steep screw, and only one turn to the right of a
lever forming the trigger guard was needed to expose
the bore. One hundred of these flintlock rifles were
manufactured in England to arm a company which Fergusson himself commanded during the American Revo-

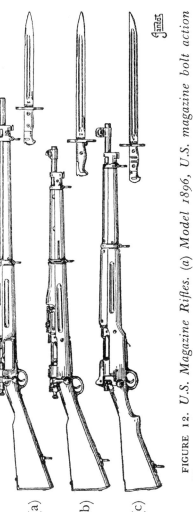

FIGURE 12. *U.S. Magazine Rifles. (a) Model 1896, U.S. magazine bolt action rifle, .30 cal. (Krag Jörgensen) (type used in Spanish-American War); (b) Model 1903, U.S. magazine bolt action rifle, .30 cal. (Springfield); (c) Model 1917, U.S. magazine bolt action rifle, .30 cal. (Enfield). [(b) and (c) are types used during World War I.]*

lutionary War. The entire company, including the commanding officer, was wiped out at Kings Mountain in 1780. The inventor's death spelled doom to a weapon well ahead of its day.

To be fair to the American and British Armies, nevertheless, we must admit that Fergusson's breechloader allowed too much gas leakage. The heat of continuous firing caused the parts to expand and the device became useless. So in 1792, when President Washington decided to establish a battalion of riflemen consisting of four companies each made up of eighty-two men, he armed the soldiers with a muzzle-loading, flintlock rifle, caliber .54. The weapon was 4 feet long, one foot shorter than the musket which, not being rifled, needed a longer barrel to guide the bullet. The contracts were issued to private riflemakers of "Kentucky rifle" fame, residing in Maryland and Pennsylvania. Each piece cost ten dollars. Other contracts were made until 1810 to trade with friendly Indian tribes.

In 1803 the secretary of war, Henry Dearborn, directed the Harpers Ferry Armory to proceed with the manufacture of four thousand rifles which differed from the preceding type chiefly in having half stocks. A rifle or a musket is said to be half stocked when its wooden stock reaches midway between the breech and the muzzle of the barrel. Because of the war with England, the government determined in 1814 to raise three additional regiments of riflemen and ordered rifles differing from the 1803 Model in that the barrel's length was reduced to 36 inches to facilitate loading. The United States Rifle, Model 1817, then came out. Its wooden stock extended nearly to the muzzle. The reader will remember that the bent stock reduced recoil effects because, having to level up and raise the forward part of the gun before receiving the backward kick, it used up some of the recoil force.

The United States Army met success with the rifle. In 1815, when we were at war with England, an English Army under General Packenham landed and attempted to take New Orleans. To do so, the English had to make a frontal attack upon the defending lines of Andrew Jackson. Packenham expected to have to cross only 100 yards under the fire of the Americans' short-range muskets. Jackson's men, however, carried rifles, and they began to decimate the enemy at a range of 300 yards. Packenham's mistake ended in Jackson's victory. This success favorably disposed our Army toward rifles, for the Ordnance Department soon adopted the United States Rifle, Model 1819. It was the invention of John H. Hall, who had patented it in 1811. It passed trials supervised by officers of the Army, and the government signed a contract in 1819 which empowered it to manufacture one thousand rifles at the Harpers Ferry Armory. In 1824, when the first contract was completed, the Army ordered another thousand rifles as well as six thousand in 1828. As a matter of fact, production continued until 1844, and Simeon North manufactured quite a few, displeasing Hall who felt that he was entitled to supervise the making of his patent rifle at the Harpers Ferry Armory. Troops used the gun in the Seminole and Blackhawk Indian Wars and in the Mexican War.

Hall's rifle, caliber .52, was a breechloader, the prin-

ciple of which was not new. The charge was placed in a
separate chamber which was hinged at its rear end and
which worked up and down. It was tilted up to insert the

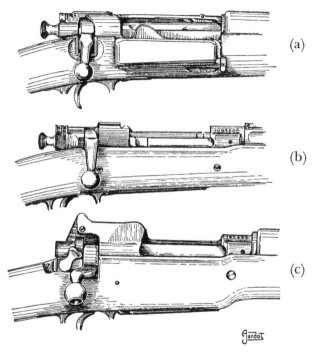

(a)

(b)

(c)

FIGURE 13. *Actions of U.S. Magazine Rifles.* (a) *Model 1896
U.S. magazine bolt action rifle, .30 cal. (Krag Jörgensen);
(b) Model 1903, U.S. magazine bolt action rifle, .30 cal.
(Springfield); (c) Model 1917, U.S. magazine bolt action rifle,
.30 cal. (Enfield).*

powder and the ball and lowered to fire. The flintlock
was attached to the movable chamber. Although gas leakage occurred, the arm was quite satisfactory. Naturally

it could not fire as heavy a charge as the solidly breeched muzzle-loaders, yet for quick firing at short range it was the best weapon of its kind.

In 1833 the Army adopted a carbine with the Hall system of breech-loading. The carbine's caliber of .69 was heavy, but its length was only 45 inches. A carbine is a shoulder weapon shorter than a rifle. Its maneuverability is essential to the work of mounted troops. Its range is somewhat shorter and its accuracy inferior to that of the longer rifle, yet both range and accuracy must be sacrificed in arming cavalry and artillery. The Hall carbine was manufactured by Simeon North of Middletown, Connecticut, and was issued to the First Regiment of Dragoons. It was the first arm accepted by the United States Army which had a percussion system of ignition. The ramrod, which was now used to clean the barrel and no longer to push the charge down through the muzzle, also served as a bayonet. The barrel was shortened and rifled in 1836, and the guns manufactured with the improvements became known as "the United States Rifle Carbine, Model 1836."

The first rifle to have a percussion lock was manufactured at the Harpers Ferry Armory and approved by an Ordnance Board in 1841. By that time the percussion system had supplanted the old flintlocks. Its discovery had been more or less accidental. Around the eighteen hundreds, when the British blockade was already gnawing at France's supply of saltpeter, a supply which the country needed to feed with powder and explosives the hungry mouths of its much-used artillery, Napoleon summoned Berthollet, the famous chemist, and asked him to find a substitute for saltpeter. Berthollet experimented with potassium chlorate ($KClO_3$) and with fulminates of mercury and silver ($CNOHg$, $CNOAg$). When even the mercury compound proved too violent by splitting the gun barrel, the French scientist gave up the search as too dangerous. It was about then that a Scottish clergyman, Alexander Forsyth, realized that Berthollet's compound could be used as a means of ignition rather than as a substitute for saltpeter. Since the compound exploded at a slight blow, Forsyth mixed the mercury fulminates with the priming powder in the pan of his old flintlock, after having removed the cover, and struck it with the hammer. The severe explosion caused the chamber to burst. The venthole was subsequently shifted to the top, yet fulminate ashes always clogged the hole. It was not until Shaw of Philadelphia screwed a hollow nipple into the top of the gun and placed on it a copper cap containing the fulminate of mercury that the discovery was made practical enough to reduce sharply the number of misfires.

Another problem bothered soldiers, namely, the difficulty of loading a ball through the muzzle of a rifled barrel. Naturally one solution was the adaptation of breech-loading systems. These allowed so much gas leakage, however, that their short range and small charge prevented their use as standard infantry weapons. The only alternative left was to ease the muzzle-loading operation. The reader should remember that rifling the bore was instituted because gunsmiths thought that the powder ashes, which befouled the bore and forestalled further loading, would fall into the grooves, thus lengthening the intervals at which the operator had to clean the barrel. Then it was accidentally discovered that spiral grooves would spin a tightly gripped ball, resulting in more accuracy. Yet in order to achieve this the soldier had to ram in a tight ball and clean the grooves if they were to spin the missiles, so that rifling, instead of making it easier, made muzzle-loading very hard.

To facilitate loading, a Frenchman by the name of Delvigne devised around 1830 a gun whose barrel narrowed at the breech to form a shoulder where the ball rested until the gunner rammed it down to cause the lead bullet to expand and fill the grooves. A few years later another Frenchman, Thouvenin, invented *le fusil à tige,* the gun with a stem. The barrel had a stem projecting from its breech to act as an anvil against which the bullet was struck with the ramrod to fill in the grooves. These two muzzle-loaders were useless, however, because once the ball had been rammed down it was deformed and its flight became too irregular. In England the Lancaster rifle, with its oval barrel and oval bullet, and the Whitworth rifle, having hexagonal barrel and bullet, achieved long distances with accuracy but were soon abandoned because powder ashes fouled the angular bore easily and made loading extremely difficult.

The Americans early recognized the advantages of the long bullet, which displaced less air and met less resistance than the round ball, and it was around 1830 that they brought out the first successful long bullet to travel in a grooved bore. People called it the "sugar loaf" because its silhouette presented rounded lines from base to point. In such a missile only the base came in contact with the walls of the barrel and the rifling indentations were so short that the long bullet was almost as easily forced down as a ball. A greased patch was placed over the muzzle and pressed down with the bullet; it acted as a gastight stopper, preventing gas leakage around the missile, and helped the grooves to grip it firmly and spin it while it also supported the cone by keeping it in the center of the barrel. In order to avoid tipping the cone, a ramrod with a cup-shaped head fitting over the bullet's point was used for muzzle-loading. The "sugar loaf" remained in use until the discovery of the Minié ball, for it was an accurate missile which often traveled over 500 yards.

In 1849 a Frenchman named Minié invented a cylindroconoidal lead bullet, the base of which had a deep taper hollow to receive an iron plug. The bullet was small enough to slide easily into the barrel. The shock of explosion pushed the plug deeper into the cavity and expanded it by spreading the sides against the walls of the barrel and into the grooves. The British adopted in 1851 a modified form known as Pritchett's blunt-nose bullet and used it in the Crimean War. It was the first time that an army carried a muzzle-loading rifle-musket as its standard weapon upon the battlefield. The British, however, were not very satisfied. Upon rapid firing, the leaden bullet, melted by the heat, left rings of metal within the barrel which it was impossible to clean. Moreover, since much of the bullet was hollow, thus lightening the material, the missile was of large size for its weight, and it displaced too much air without having the momentum to meet it. The United States Army experimented with Captain Minié's elongated bullet at the Harpers Ferry Armory where Mr. Burton, the assistant master armorer, found that the iron or wooden plug was not necessary to expand the base, for the gases' pressure would do it. In 1855 the Minié bullet was adopted, and the rifles manufactured in 1841 were reamed up and rerifled to caliber .58 to use the new missile.

It was again in 1855 that new cavalry regiments were formed and armed with the United States Rifled-Carbine, Model 1855, 36.75 inches long, of caliber .58, using the Minié elongated and pointed bullet. Over one thousand of the straight percussion carbines came out of the Springfield Armory. A new arm appeared in 1855, the rifled-musket. About five thousand of the flintlock muskets available were altered by Remington to incorporate the Maynard tape-lock primer similar to that used for the pistol (Chapter One) with the exception that the roll contained fifty primers instead of the pistol's twenty-five. The length was that of a musket, 59 inches; the barrel was rifled and the caliber reduced to .58 to use the Minié bullet. Thus the new weapon was a combination of the rifle and the musket, a compromise designed to unite the merits of both arms and to achieve uniformity in the Army's ordnance. The designation of rifled-musket was retained until 1873. Jefferson Davis, who was then secretary of war, also fostered the adoption of a pure rifle in 1855, 49.30 inches in length, equipped with a saber bayonet having a brass handle.

All the guns, however, with the exception of Hall's breech-loading carbines, were muzzle-loaders with all the implications as to slowness and encumbrance. Naturally there had been successful systems of breech-loading, as the names of Fergusson and Hall testify. For instance, in 1848, an American named Christian Sharps invented a breech-loading rifle which became the invaluable tool of many pioneers. The hinged breechblock worked up and down so that the operator could insert the paper cartridge, containing ball and powder ignited by a percussion cap, directly into the chamber. The charge was not as large as that of a muzzle-loader and the caliber was only .52; yet "Sharps' Old Reliable," as it was called, was remarkable for its range, accuracy, and hitting power. John Brown's men carried it when they went into action. During the Civil War it was issued to Northern troops, especially to cavalrymen, and it was still fighting Indians in 1870 after it had been adapted to use the metallic cartridge.

Although it worked quickly, Sharps' breech action allowed too much gas leakage and backflash. Indeed, that was the bane of all breechloaders, and it was to remedy this defect that George W. Morse patented on October 28, 1856, the first small-arms cartridge and proposed a new system of breech closing which both Army and Navy boards accepted. The "fixed cartridge" consisted of a metallic cylindrical case with a rimmed base; it encased the Minié bullet, the powder charge, and the primer, which was a percussion cap fixed in the center of the base. When the pinheaded plug struck the cap's seat in the middle of the base the cap detonated and caused the charge to explode. The pinheaded plug was pushed by a hammer upon release of the trigger and it traveled horizontally inside the breechblock to strike the center-fire cartridge. The breechblock, or rather the breech-closing device, was hinged at the rear so that it worked up and down to allow loading the chambered barrel. Morse's system was the precursor of both the bolt action and the metallic, center-fire cartridge. It was well ahead of its day. The inventor joined the rebel cause at the beginning of the Civil War and established himself in Greenville, South Carolina, to manufacture arms for the Confederacy.

The reader must not suppose, however, that Morse was entirely original in his boltlike system and his center-fire, metallic cartridge. He may have been influenced by the trials which went on in Europe, especially in Prussia and France. For instance, in 1836 a German gunsmith, Johann Nikolaus von Dreyse, who had worked for many years in the gunshop of Pauli, a Swiss arms maker established in Paris, patented in Prussia what is now considered as the first "needle gun." Pauli had manufactured weapons for Napoleon, and in 1827 he had made a paper cartridge with a paper percussion cap placed at the base of the bullet. To fire this cartridge, a needle struck through the powder to the percussion cap which detonated. Von Dreyse perfected the system. The needle was actioned by a hammer, traveled horizontally through the breech, and lay within an iron rod or bolt which exposed the breech when drawn back toward the operator by means of a lever, so that the paper cartridge might be inserted into the chamber. When the bolt was pushed back and locked by bringing the lever down, it pushed the cartridge into the chamber to prevent any leakage. Although the gun had a shorter range than a muzzle-loading rifle, its rate of fire was so rapid that the Prussian Army adopted it in 1841.

The Prussians used their rifles with great success in their war with Austria in 1866. Yet there was one defect which often made the gun useless. The thin steel needle had to pass through the powder to hit the percussion cap at the bullet's base; therefore, the needle was still in the powder when the explosion took place. The high heat corroded and softened the needle which often broke as a result, making it necessary to change the entire bolt. To remedy this, the French found it preferable to place the percussion cap at the base of the paper cartridge instead of upon the wad between the powder and the bullet. The Prussians had thought that such an arrangement would start the ignition at the base of the cartridge and would force many grains of powder out before they had had a chance to explode. The French disproved this theory and obtained a needle rifle more accurate and of longer range. They reduced the caliber from .66 to .43 and added the de Bange gas stopper, a rubber ring placed within the breech which, because of the pressure of the expanding gases, was compressed and had to spread by pushing upon the barrel's walls, thus preventing gas leakage. After many shots, however, the heat of firing hardened the rubber which, having lost its elasticity, became useless as a gas stopper. This was known as the Chassepot gun. Thus we can see that Morse might have had some knowledge of the needle gun.

Morse's center-fire, metallic cartridge also had precursors. For instance, the Frenchman Lefaucheux, in

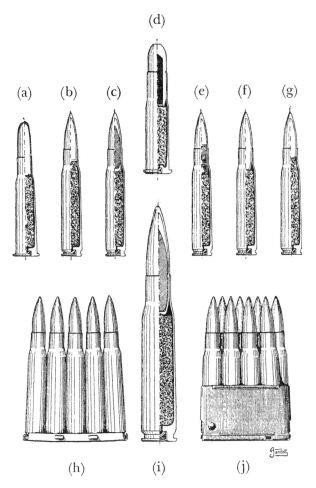

FIGURE 14. *Small-arms Cartridges.* (a) *Model 1896, .30-cal.
ball cartridge;* (b) *Model 1906, .30-cal. ball cartridge;*
(c) *Model 1917, .30-cal. armor-piercing cartridge;* (d) *Model
1920, 11mm. incendiary cartridge;* (e) *Model 1918, .30-cal.
tracer cartridge;* (f) *M1, .30-cal. ball cartridge;* (g) *M2, .30-cal.
ball cartridge;* (h) *clip of five cartridges for rifles, Model 1903
and 1917;* (i) *Model 1923, .50-cal. armor-piercing cartridge;*
(j) *clip for rifle M1 (Garand).*

1838, devised a metallic cartridge for his double-barreled gun with the barrels hinged to the breech so that they might be dropped to insert the cartridges. This system only survived in the shotgun. The next metallic cartridge came in 1847, the invention of Houiller, a Paris gunmaker, who used a thin copper cylinder closed at the rear to hold the powder and a bullet protruding at the orifice. The copper case, stretched by the explosion, pressed against the barrel walls and prevented gas leakage. The expansion was not produced by the heat but by the pressure of exploding gases, for copper has a certain elasticity not found in other metals. After the explosion the copper contracted sufficiently to allow the extraction of the case. A pin protruded at the side near the base. When the hammer struck it, the pin hit and set off the percussion cap within the case. To manufacture the case was expensive and dangerous since anything might strike the pin accidentally. It was also slowly loaded, for the pin, to be struck by the hammer, had to be placed perpendicularly.

Houiller soon changed his system and produced the rim-fire cartridge, in which the detonating material was spread as evenly as possible around the base's rim. Martin's adaptation of the rim-fire cartridge was used extensively in the United States after 1865. As its copper case was not strong enough to withstand heavy charges, brass was substituted. Thus Morse's center-fire cartridge, which was a combination of the needle gun's paper cartridge and of Houiller's metallic case, was discarded as being too extravagant.

There were many attempts besides that of Morse, just

before and during the Civil War, to speed the rate of
fire by the use of some sort of breechloader. The Sharps
carbine, which mounted troops used widely during the
conflict, has already been discussed. Of course, there was
Colt's rifle with a revolving chambered cylinder similar
to that of the repeating pistol; although the Army issued the arm to some troops, it did not look upon
the weapon favorably because of excessive gas leakage.
Around 1860 Union mounted troops began to use thousands of Spencer's repeating carbine, which could fire
sixteen shots per minute and which increased a soldier's
firing power to that of six men. Seven rim-fire cartridges
fitted through an opening at the butt into the magazine, a tube running lengthwise through the stock up to
the chamber which could hold an eighth cartridge. It
was a breechloader with a block moving up and down to
close the breech. While there remained cartridges in the
magazine, the soldier could reload without removing the
gun from his shoulder by merely swinging backward a
lever situated under the barrel just as in the Sharps
carbine. The lever extracted and ejected the empty case
and inserted a fresh cartridge. The hammer had to be
cocked by the thumb after each shot. The bullets were,
of course, short, pointed projectiles, and the copper case,
too weak to withstand heavy charges, contained only
forty-five grains of black powder, thus shortening the
range. Another defect was that the copper cases often
stuck to the chamber after a long period of fire.

The Henry repeater was a carbine which the Northern troops also used late in the Civil War. It was a
strictly American weapon, a breechloader, using the bolt

system of closing the breech, probably in imitation of Morse's efforts. The magazine tube was attached under the barrel (a device used by Kropatschek of Austria in the eighteen seventies); it contained fifteen copper-cased, rim-fire cartridges inserted into the tube through its front end. The lever underneath the barrel threw out the empty case, loaded fresh ammunition into the chamber, and cocked the hammer. Later on it was improved by King to use a center-fire cartridge with a heavier charge, and it became well known as the "Winchester." In spite of the Winchester's success in South America, where it helped Chile to defeat Peru and Bolivia in the War of the Pacific in 1879, the United States Army was loath to adopt such a repeater, because the shifting of the cartridges in the tubular magazine as they were fired affected the gun's balance and the aim in rapid fire. Military experts also feared that a magazine supply of fifteen cartridges would lead the soldiers to fire extravagantly. Since the cartridges were of high caliber and heavy, soldiers might not be able to carry a sufficient amount, and to replenish their stores during a battle would present a difficult problem to supply organizations.

On the eve of the Civil War, therefore, the standard weapon of our infantry—and the infantry by far outweighed in importance the carbine-armed cavalry and artillery—was the muzzle-loading, tape-priming riflemusket, Model 1855. Maynard's tape primer had met with such opposition in all the Services because of its impracticality that late in 1860 a new model was determined upon which discarded Maynard's system and returned to the percussion cap. In all other particulars it resembled the previous type, firing a .58-caliber paper cartridge which enclosed the Minié bullet. Production had hardly started on it when the Civil War broke out. The government contracted with Colt, with the Amoskeag Manufacturing Company, and with Lamson, Goodnow, and Yale, along with many others, to manufacture the rifled-musket, the pattern of which was slightly changed in 1863. The war placed such strain on the resources of the Ordnance Department that it had to import muskets from Europe.

At the end of the Civil War, in 1865, when the United States faced a possible war with Napoleon III, the emperor of the French, as a result of the latter's meddling in Mexican affairs, the Ordnance Department found that if we were to keep our Army on an equal footing with European forces we would have to adopt a breech-loading infantry weapon. Breech-loading had already traveled far, and its capacities in rapid fire overshadowed such considerations as gas leakage, smaller charges, and lower muzzle velocity (the speed at which a bullet travels when it leaves the muzzle). In 1864 a British ordnance board had ordered that all the Enfield rifles be converted to breech-loading until it could recommend a new rifle. In the same way the United States Army had five thousand of the muzzle-loading rifle-muskets used during the Civil War converted to breech-loading. E. S. Allin, the master armorer at the Springfield Armory, devised an expedient in which the breech was milled open and a hinged bolt was fixed by means of two screws to the top of the barrel in front of the breech opening. The percussion hammer was retained so that the firing pin had to slide through the bolt on a slant to strike the cartridge. On the right side of the barrel was a ratchet operating the extractor. The caliber was .58 and the rifle fired Martin's copper, rim-fire cartridge, the first metallic cartridge adopted for the entire Army.

The caliber of this rifle was reduced during the following year from .58 to .50 by brazing a tube inside the barrel. A U-shaped spring replaced the previous ratchet-action extractor. Moreover, finally rediscovering Morse's invention, the Army adopted a center-fire cartridge to take the place of rim-fire ammunition; that is, instead of spreading the detonating or priming chemical over the case's rim a percussion cap was placed in the center of the case's base. Besides, the primer needed an anvil to explode when struck by the firing pin. Around 1870, to reduce the cost, General Berdan of the United States Army suggested that cases be stamped out of a single piece of brass with an anvil at the base of the primer or percussion cap cavity in the case. By 1885 the reloadable or crimp primer was used on all cartridges manufactured for the Services.

Improvements were made on the Allin alteration rifle in 1868, 1869, and 1870. Somehow the need was felt for a new model. In 1870, for instance, upon the recommendation of a naval ordnance board, the Navy ordered the manufacture of ten thousand rifles at the Springfield Armory. The caliber was .50, the gun a single-shot breechloader using the Remington rolling-block action. These ten thousand rifles were sold, incidentally, to France during the Franco-Prussian War of 1870, because the rear sight was placed in a wrong position and could not be repaired without weakening the barrel. The Army had some experimental Remington rifles made as well as a limited number using the Ward-Burton system. This was a single-loader, bolt-action arm. The rear of the bolt was partly threaded to lock it when it was closed in the firing position. The bolthead was movable and contained the extractor and the ejector. The bolt had a lever and resembled the Prussian and French needle guns and even our World War I rifle. The Army found, however, that the Allin alteration type was still the best. In 1873 the caliber of this rifle was reduced to .45 and it remained the basic model for almost twenty years.

On November 21, 1877, Congress passed an act for the selection of a magazine rifle to arm the Services. A board of officers convened and selected the Hotchkiss gun the following year. The rifle had a capacity of six cartridges, one in the chamber and five in a tubular magazine located in the butt of the stock. The magazine was loaded through a trap in the butt plate. The cartridges were in a row, the last one pushing the others forward because of the pressure of a coil spring with a pistonhead. Each cartridge came successively into the receiver through a hole at its rear end under the bolt, and it was fed into the chamber by pushing the bolt and locking it. Having a caliber of .45, the gun was around 48 inches long and bore a triangular rod bayonet. It was manufactured at the Springfield Armory, but was never used extensively by the Army.

The Army made an attempt in 1882 to do away with the carbine for mounted troops by shortening the standard rifle so that the cavalry and the artillery might use the same weapon as the infantry. The advantages of such a system in the matter of uniformity of military supplies would have been enormous. Fifty of those short rifles were issued to the mounted troops at Fort Leavenworth for trials. Although the attempt failed because the length could not be sufficiently reduced, the idea was not forgotten. In the same year the Army tried another magazine, bolt-action arm, caliber .45, made on the Chaffee-Reece system. It had a tubular magazine in the butt of the stock, the magazine being fed through a trap in the butt plate. Within the magazine were two racks having alternate indentations into which fitted the cartridges' rim. As the bolt opened, one rack moved sufficiently high to allow a cartridge shouldered by one of its indentations to slip into that of the opposite rack. The closing of the bolt caused the opposite rack to move also and, with each working of the bolt or as one shot was fired, all the cartridges in the magazine ascended to the next indentation on their way to the chamber. In 1884 a model of the United States Rifle came out with the "Buffington wind-gauge sight," the first sight used by the Army to enable soldiers to make corrections for the drift caused by the wind. The last of those .45-caliber rifles were made in 1889.

In 1886, France adopted a magazine rifle proposed by Colonel Lebel of the French Army. It was remarkable in that it was the first arm to have a caliber as small as 8mm. (.31). This small caliber was made possible by Lebel's use of a cartridge having a charge not of black powder but of smokeless powder invented by the French chemist Vieille. Of course, Vieille had had the work of previous scientists to lead him to his discovery. The French chemist Bracconnet, for instance, found in 1832 that vegetable starch, upon being dipped into nitric acid (HNO_3) and washed, gives a substance which explodes violently upon concussion. About the same time his countryman Pelouze discovered that he could substitute cotton for vegetable starch, although the resulting explosive was too sensitive and violent. In 1845, Schönbein sold "guncotton," as it was called, to Austro-Hungary. Twenty years later wood fiber was treated with nitric acid to produce the Schultze powder. Cotton was adopted, however, because it is almost pure cellulose and, when dipped into nitric acid, gives nitrocellulose.

It was found that guncotton increased in explosive power in relation to the length of time it remained in the nitric acid. As a result, manufacturers adopted a middle course, leaving the substance in solution only long enough for it to acquire a moderate explosive force. The guncotton was then washed and became white and fluffy. Nevertheless, it was still too violent, for upon combustion it produced carbon monoxide (CO), carbon dioxide (CO_2), nitrogen (N), and steam (H_2O), gases three times as voluminous as those set forth by black powder (a physical mixture of saltpeter, sulphur, and charcoal). It was then discovered that if the guncotton (nitrocellulose) were dissolved and nitroglycerin, a violent explosive by itself, were added, the resulting mixture would become a moderate, even a slow, explosive. Sometimes nitrocellulose or nitroglycerin is used alone, although a mixture of the two with the possible addition of further deterrents such as graphite or heavy oils is preferred by most nations.

Contrary to what its name implies, smokeless powder is neither smokeless nor powder. It does produce smoke, even though in quantities so imperceptible that it does not reveal the position from which a soldier fires. Moreover, it is granulated into cylindrical pellets of equal size, perforated through with one hole for small-arms ammunition, with six holes for artillery. In order to ensure even combustion, the perforations must be regular and the molds used in the manufacture of grains are unusually exact. The fact that smokeless powder produces little smoke, however, is not its important quality. To be sure, it is easier to store and handle than black powder; it will burn quietly when lighted in the open; a direct blow or near-by shock will not cause it to explode unless it is hot, which is one reason why smokeless powder needs a strong primer; finally, it is not affected by moisture in the same degree that black powder is.

Yet, although these qualities stand out, they are not the transcending property which brought about in arms changes greater, perhaps, than those ushered in by the metallic cartridge. Being a slow explosive, smokeless powder burned over a length of time. The time of the explosion was stretched so that the gases first started the bullet slowly on its way, increasing its speed as the gases' volume multiplied until the projectile reached a maximum, vertiginous pace near the muzzle. The slow start gave the bullet a chance to set firmly into the grooves, and the turn of the rifling was gradually accentuated until the bullet revolved upon its own axis so fast that the spinning maintained the speed and, therefore, the hitting power of a missile over a range undreamed of previously.

When black powder exploded, and sometimes much of it had no time to explode, the gases hit the barrel's walls and then forced the bullet out at the first impact. It was only after the bullet had left the muzzle that the gases reached the forward part of the barrel, that the remaining powder burned without increasing the speed of the departing bullet. Thus much powder was wasted, since range and accuracy depended upon postponing the effects of the law of gravity and of air resistance by decreasing the time of flight. In other words, the faster a bullet reaches its goal, the lower is the trajectory, the better the accuracy. Therefore, everything hinges upon the speed at which a projectile leaves the muzzle, that is, the muzzle velocity. One could, naturally, increase the speed by multiplying the black powder charge, but the expedient resulted in such recoil strength and in the use of such heavy weapons to withstand the explosion that it had to be abandoned. To decrease the amount of lead did not help either, since it is the diameter, and not the bullet's weight, which influences air resistance. Besides, lessening the weight meant less hitting power, while the speed remained constant.

Bullets similar in shape and diameter, when traveling at a speed of 1,350 feet or over per second, meet air resistance in proportion to the square of their velocity. Since a bullet half the weight of another must travel twice as fast to have the same hitting power, of two bullets similar in shape and diameter, the lighter one will meet four times the air resistance that the heavier meets, with resulting weakness and inaccuracy. The only way to decrease air resistance is to lower the diameter, lengthen the bullet, and reduce the caliber. Yet the rate of rotation or spinning must be increased in proportion to the decrease in diameter to ensure stability in flight. This means that the twist of rifling has to be sharper, that the lead bullet has to be hardened with zinc, antimony, or tin so that the projectiles may not tear through the barrel without following the grooves. Thus by 1885 it had become possible to reduce the caliber to .45 and even to .40. Nevertheless, without smokeless powder the reduction of the caliber to .30 or .25 would never have occurred, for it was smokeless powder which, with its slowly starting explosion and the bullet's initial sluggishness, permitted the leaden missile to grip the grooves firmly and to follow their sharp twist in spite of its everincreasing pace; which, because it used completely the gases' propelling force, raised the muzzle velocity to new heights and lessened the recoil shock by making it more gradual and by giving a chance to the stock to absorb it.

In 1890 a board of officers convened in New York to recommend a suitable magazine rifle of caliber .30. Inasmuch as a small-caliber rifle was useless without an adequate supply of smokeless powder, the board could not report upon a rifle before 1892, when American producers hit upon the formula which European powers held in secrecy. The board examined all the inventions of domestic and foreign gunmakers in addition to the official weapons of other countries. It classified these weapons in two categories: first, the repeating rifles which could not be used as single-loaders while the magazine was filled; second, those which could be used as single-loaders with a full magazine. The board favored the last type and adopted the Krag-Jörgensen, the invention of Captain O. Krag of the Royal Arms Factory at Kongsberg, Norway. E. Jörgensen of the same city assisted him. The rifle was a magazine arm loading through a gate on the right side of the receiver at the breech. The cartridges had a rimmed base; they were of caliber .30. Production did not begin until 1894, because Congress passed an act requiring trials for American inventions before the Krag-Jörgensen could be adopted. Soldiers of the Regular Army used the gun during the Spanish-American War, while the militia and the volunteers carried the 1873 model.

At the turn of the nineteenth century, European rifles, all of the magazine and bolt-action type, could be classified after two models: the German Mauser and the Austrian Mannlicher. The Mauser gun was loaded by means of a charger holding five cartridges which were forced down into the magazine with the thumb. The bolt contained a firing pin, a spring, and an extractor, all of which were inserted at the rear end of the bolt. The Mannlicher was loaded by means of a clip remaining in the magazine as long as it contained cartridges. The firing pin consisted of two separate pieces and was inserted at the front end of the bolt. This bolt was not as strong and simple as that of the Mauser, but it was cheaper to replace its broken firing pin. In 1903 the Army chose the Mauser type of rifle which the Spanish troops had used so effectively during the Spanish-American War, and the gun was designated as the United States Magazine Rifle, Model 1903. It is commonly called "the Springfield" after a custom in this country of naming a rifle after the place where it has been produced, in this case the Springfield Armory. It was first equipped with a rod-type bayonet, and the breech was chambered to receive the 220-grain, Krag-type, blunt-nose bullet in a rimless case.

Two years later Theodore Roosevelt ordered that a knife bayonet be substituted for the rod-bayonet, because the latter broke too easily. In 1906 these rifles were rechambered for the 1906 rimless service cartridge which was copied from the German Spitzer 150-grain, flat-base, pointed-nose bullet encased in a cupronickel jacket. This bullet was streamlined in 1924 by having its base tapering slightly to meet less air resistance, and it became known as the "boat-tail" bullet. The Model 1903 A1, which only came out in 1926, differed from the other gun in having a pistol grip stock. Since the length of the Springfield did not exceed 43 inches, the arm was issued to mounted troops as well as to the infantry, and the carbine was discarded.

The first World War caught us with an insufficient supply of the 1903 rifle and with no private gunmaker tooled up to go into production. Therefore, we adopted the British Model 1914, the Lee-Enfield, reducing its caliber from the British .303 to fit the United States service cartridge, caliber .30. These rifles were issued to our troops as Model 1917, and over 2,500,000 were manufactured.

The United States Automatic Pistol, Model 1918, was a secret weapon misnamed to conceal its real nature from foreign agents. It was the invention of J. D. Pedersen. The "Pedersen device," as it was called, could convert an ordinary rifle into a light machine gun, thus increasing tremendously a soldier's firing power. The operator removed the standard bolt from his rifle and replaced it with a boltlike device which fired the small cartridges of a clip placed over the receiver. The instrument was carried in a metal holster attached to the soldier's cartridge belt. The government destroyed most of the Pedersen devices a few years after the first World War to prevent gangsters from coming into possession of what they could transform into a formidable submachine gun.

In 1936 the United States Army adopted the Garand rifle as the new standard weapon for the Services. The arm was developed by J. C. Garand, a French-Canadian employed at the Springfield Armory, who had been experimenting since 1920. The rifle is a semiautomatic weapon, that is, one shot is fired by each squeeze of the trigger. It is fed by means of a clip holding eight cartridges of caliber .30. It is a gas-operated, self-loading shoulder arm stemming from the Browning automatic rifle, which will be treated in the next chapter. A piston tube is situated under the barrel and communicates with it near the muzzle. When a cartridge is fired and the bullet clears the muzzle, the gases generated by the explosion rush from the barrel partly into the piston tube, thus pushing backward the piston, which in turn opens the bolt, extracts and ejects the empty cartridge case,

then closes and locks the bolt, which shoves a fresh cartridge into the chamber, when the gases escape from the
tube and allow the piston to return to its normal position. The wooden parts are three in number: the
pistol-gripped stock which fits the hollow of the shoulder; the rear hand guard which leaves the barrel un-
covered so that the cool air may nullify the bad effects
of heat produced by continuous fire; and the front hand
guard which covers the barrel to prevent the soldier
from burning himself when he holds that part of the
gun with his left hand.

The Garand does not differ very much in general appearance from the Springfield 1903 rifle. It has a weight
of 8.94 pounds and the sling and the bayonet add another pound. The entire length of the gun is 43 inches.
The barrel alone stands 22.30 inches. The bore has four
grooves with a uniform, right-hand twist accomplishing
one turn every 10 inches. The rifle has a muzzle velocity
of 2,760 per second and a maximum range of 5,500
yards. The Garand is not quite as accurate as the Springfield, which sharpshooters still prefer. This is not a defect, however; tactics have so changed that it is no
longer necessary to cut a twig a mile distant with a
bullet. The emphasis is upon the rate of fire, and the
Garand is remarkable from that point of view since a
soldier can deliver fifty shots a minute. The Garand's
recoil shock is softer than that of the Springfield so that
it does not tire a man as another gun would. The reader
should not conclude that our new rifle is not accurate,
for it is sufficiently dependable to fulfill any mission.

The Garand is naturally a better weapon than the

Mauser, which Germany used during the first World War and with which she is fighting the present conflict. The Mauser and our Springfield are much alike, and they are not as well adapted to modern warfare as our new weapon. The Garand rifle is manufactured by the

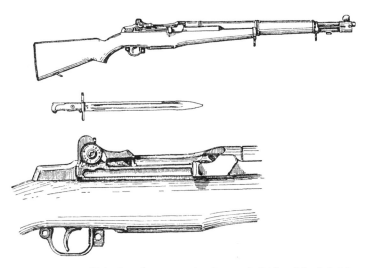

FIGURE 15. *U.S. Semiautomatic Garand Rifle, Model M1 (1936), .30 cal.; Model 1905 knife bayonet; and Model M1 Garand (1936) action.*

Springfield Armory and the Winchester Arms Company of New Haven, Connecticut. We have about two hundred thousand Garand rifles on hand. They are being issued to the troops as fast as they are turned out on a priority basis, our regular troops being served first. Production is so satisfactory that our entire armed forces will have Garands within a year. In addition, we possess some eight hundred thousand Model 1903 Springfields which are by no means obsolete. Approximately 2,500,-000 Model 1917 (Lee-Enfield) guns remained from the first World War, many of which have been recently allocated to various state guards. Thus we do not face any shortage of rifles.

During the last few years there has been a tendency in some European countries to furnish soldiers with rifles that are indeed small machine guns, or that can be used as such in case of an emergency developing a fast rate of fire. For instance, our Garand rifle strongly resembles the Browning light machine gun, and although it is only semiautomatic the soldier's work is limited to feeding the weapon and to squeezing the trigger for each shot. The Army has not adopted a fully automatic weapon as the standard tool of the infantry because it prefers the simplicity, strength, maneuverability, and light weight of a semiautomatic rifle to the complexity and bulk of a full automatic gun.

An automatic weapon which can fire fifty rounds of ammunition in a fraction of a minute has drawbacks limiting its use to that of one man in each squad. It will be remembered that recoil action has two effects: first, the recoil's backward force thrusts the stock of the gun against the operator's shoulder; secondly, much of the recoil action is absorbed when the bent stock attempts to level up the piece by raising the forward part of the barrel. Both effects, the blow against the shoulder and the rise of the barrel, are cumulative when the rate of fire is that of an automatic gun. Should a soldier fire fifty rounds in a fraction of a second upon one squeeze of the trigger, the recoil blow would be so strong and painful that he would shrink and spoil his aim, and the barrel's upward surge would be so powerful that he would not be able to keep the gun pointing toward the general direction of the target. Thus the great majority of his bullets would be wasted and his shoulder would be too bruised to repeat the ordeal. The soldier can, of course, fire without aiming, but the sacrifice in accuracy is too great to make the operation effective. To increase the stability of an automatic rifle, its weight is often raised and a bipod added; yet these changes make the weapon too cumbersome for general use.

There is, moreover, a limit to the number of shots, even from a simple rifle, which a strong man can fire. Whenever a soldier shoots over fifty rounds within a few hours his shoulder becomes more and more bruised with each additional shot, and there comes a time, varying according to the individual's strength, when he will shrink upon firing in expectation of the recoil blow. Since this shrinking back spoils the aim, the man never hits his target and his gun becomes a useless tool. Therefore, inasmuch as a soldier's effective firing power is limited by his own physical endurance rather than by the type of weapon he has or the difficulty of keeping him supplied with ammunition, it would be futile to give him an automatic rifle with which he cannot aim without rendering his shoulder useless after a few minutes of action. Naturally there are times when a large volume of fire is needed, and in case of such an emergency each squad has a man armed with an automatic weapon. This compromise has allowed the Army to keep the rifle with all its advantages without having to give up the large volume of fire afforded by automatic arms.

The tendency toward automatic weapons has even been more marked for the use of troops with special duties and needs. For instance, cavalrymen or parachutists often meet enemy forces in superior quantity, and they need weapons which will give them tremendous firing power and which will be light and maneuverable. Range and accuracy can be sacrificed to some degree, because those troops seldom engage the enemy at a range exceeding 300 yards. Thus, even though the rifle still remains the arm of the average soldier, the need for an increased volume of fire has brought about the introduction of weapons which perform most of the firing operations automatically.

The latest official attitude is well illustrated by the fact that Secretary of War Stimson announced at a recent press conference that the Army will test exhaustively models of two carbines. One of these will eventually replace almost all .45 caliber service pistols now in use, and, according to Secretary Stimson, the adoption of this carbine will be "the most significant step in the change of weapons in the Army that has taken place."

According to an article in the August 2, 1941, issue of the *Army and Navy Journal*, all infantry officers below the rank of major, all noncommissioned officers, and a large majority of enlisted men who are now armed with pistols will ultimately use this new weapon instead; it will also be employed to advantage by the cavalry, artillery, engineers, armored force, parachute troops, and other branches. A weapon designed for men whose duties make carrying the regular, heavier rifle practically impossible, the new arm will increase the number of rifles in an infantry regiment by about 50 per cent.

Commercial manufacturers have made six models, the Ordnance Department one. Engineering tests of the seven models have been made by the Ordnance Department. These tests eliminated five of the models, with two others coming up to specifications. One of the latter was produced by a commercial concern, and the other, described as the "little brother" of the Garand M1 rifle, was the product of the Ordnance Department. Both are to receive service tests at the Aberdeen Proving Ground. These will be carried out by men from the Infantry School at Ft. Benning, Georgia, and veterans as well as recruits will subject the new arms to all types of weather conditions. After the roughest sort of treatment the carbines will be cleaned with only the most elementary equipment. The article goes on to say that before a standard type of carbine is selected other models may be submitted for tests.

The new arm will be shorter than the Springfield or the Garand—by 8 inches. It will weigh 5 pounds, including magazine and sling (4 pounds less than the Springfield or Garand). The following are some of its other characteristics, subject to change, of course:

Caliber—.30 caliber, with 110-grain bullet similar to .38 caliber pistol bullet, but with considerably more striking power. Ammunition may not be interchanged with that of Springfield or Garand.

Feed—two sizes of clips may be used, one holding twenty cartridges and one holding ten cartridges.

Length—an over-all length of 36 inches; barrel, 18 inches. This compares with 43 inches over-all length for both the Springfield and Garand, whose barrels are 23 inches long.

Method of Carrying—equipped with a regular service rifle sling, the new weapons will be carried slung until ready to be used.

Range—effective ranges up to 300 yards.

Sights—aperture type—set for 100 and 300 yards. (No intermediate adjustments necessary.)

Type—shoulder weapons, semiautomatic. Both types to be tested are gas-operated on the same principle as the Garand but differ in certain other functional respects.

An infantry regiment is now composed of 2,099 men armed with the service rifle and 1,181 men armed with the pistol. Such a regiment in the future would rearm 944 additional men with the carbine. This would make a total of 3,043 rifles—M1 and light—and would reduce the number of pistols to 237. About 175,000 men in the infantry alone—machine gunners, ammunition carriers, mortar men, officers and noncommissioned officers, administrative and communications personnel—will receive the carbine in place of the pistol. It will also be issued to proportionate numbers in the other branches of the Service.

The fighting potentialities of the units in the forward area will be greatly increased since more than 600 of the 944 light rifles that will be added to the infantry regiment will go into that area. All the officers and men of the Heavy Weapons Company, for example, have been using the service pistol for personal defense. Now six out of eight men in each machine-gun squad will be equipped with the carbine. Only the gunner and the assistant gunner, who must carry the machine gun and its heavy tripod, will have pistols. Thus, even if its gun is knocked out, the squad may continue to act as a fighting unit by means of this new arrangement. The carbine will also enable the unit to preserve its prescribed fire power, since it could continue firing at its target while the other members of the crew deal with any incidental attack. The most carefully concocted fire plans may be upset by a machine gun being taken off its assigned mission merely to defend the gun position and the crew.

The rear areas will also be affected by use of the new rifle. These areas are now predominantly equipped with pistols, which are of little use except in hand-to-hand fighting. If the administrative and supply troops are suddenly attacked by low-flying airplanes or rapidly advancing ground forces, their position will be immeasurably bettered by use of the new weapon. It is planned to arm approximately 300 of the men in a regimental rear area with the rifle, releasing a large proportion of the security troops for service in the line.

The carbine will be an important factor in promoting high morale, for the men carrying it will feel more secure and their leaders can instill more confidence in the men since in a crisis they could join in a fire fight. In addition, a troop leader armed with a rifle is not as conspicuous as one with a pistol, and hence is not as likely to be seen by snipers.

The need for a more effective weapon for protection of the crews of supporting infantry weapons and others armed with the pistol has long been felt, even though it was realized that a new type of ammunition would have to be carried. An enemy rifleman 100 yards away would have a great advantage over a man armed with a pistol, which has an effective range of only 50 yards. No wonder, then, that this new weapon is regarded by veteran infantry officers as a "dream come true."

CHAPTER FOUR

MACHINE GUNS

SHOULD THE reader ever glance over a standard dictionary and come upon the word "machine gun," he would see that it is defined as "an automatic gun using small-arms ammunition for rapid continuous firing." Upon further analysis of the definition he would find that it can be divided into three parts, or rather that it is composed of three sections which set out the origin of the machine gun, its purpose, and the means of accomplishing that purpose. First, the machine gun uses small-arms ammunition, the same cartridges which feed a rifle. In other words, the early types of machine guns were not inventions in their own right: they were not built as a particular means of using powder, but were intended to shoot the musket's leaden ball. The earliest versions stemmed from the musket, for they constituted a new way of using an established weapon rather than coming out as an entirely new arm. Secondly, the purpose of the machine gun is to secure a rapid and continuous fire. Thirdly, the means of achieving such a firing power lies in making the gun automatic in some manner or other. Thus the earliest attempts at building anything like a machine gun were merely new methods of using muskets so that a rapid fire, as regular and continuous as possible, might be attained—new methods which consisted of eliminating some of the steps of the loading and firing cycle to be performed by the soldier.

Pedro Navarro made the first attempt to use a primitive type of machine gun in a major engagement, the Battle of Ravenna in 1512 between the Spaniards and the French. He placed in front of his foot soldiers thirty carts, on each of which were installed several heavy harquebuses. This type of weapon was developed on the Continent, where it became known as the "orgue" or "organ gun," largely because the barrels of the several muskets mounted on the frame of a wheeled carriage resembled the pipes of an organ. From the carriage's frame protruded strong, lengthy spears to protect the gunners from enemy assault. The idea was used as late as the American Civil War when the "volley guns" of Billinghurst and Requa fired metallic cartridges from twenty-five barrels using a primer train as a means of ignition. The only reminder of these guns is the double-barreled hunting piece still in use today and also the new multibarreled antiaircraft machine guns.

The germ of a more fertile device was the use of many chambers revolving around an axis. During the eighteenth century the French developed the idea whereby an average of eight barrels revolved around an axis so that each one was fired by a common flintlock through a common touchhole. The London gunsmith Nock manufactured some of these guns for the British Army as late as 1807. Samuel Colt adopted the system for his revolver and his revolving rifle. Little of the operation, however, was mechanical, and the only loading step whose reduction led to greater firing speed was the priming. Thus the machine gun had to wait until the discovery of a new breech-loading system for further progress.

In 1862, Dr. Richard J. Gatling of Chicago invented the first successful machine gun. It consisted of ten paral-

FIGURE 16. *U.S. Gatling gun, .30 cal., Model 1895.*

lel rifled barrels revolving in a circle around a fixed, central axis. Behind each barrel was the reloading and ejecting mechanism into which metallic case loaders, caliber .58 (the reader should remember that it was the standard rifle caliber at the time), falling from their own weight, were dropped from a hopper situated above the gun. An attendant at the rear of the gun turned the crank which caused the barrels to revolve and to pass the breech mechanism successively, the top barrel being fired while the others performed a step in the cycle of ejecting the empty cartridge case, receiving a fresh cartridge, and inserting it into the chamber. The Gatling gun was capable of firing two hundred shots per minute, and there was no difficulty about cooling off barrels heated by continuous fire, for each barrel was given a chance to cool before firing its next shot. The principal handicap to the wide use of the Gatling gun was the excessive weight of the mechanism and the resulting necessity of mounting the gun on a conspicuous horse-drawn carriage. The United States Army looked upon the weapon with ill-favor, and when Gatling gave several demonstrations upon the battlefield during the Civil War he had his own employees operate his machine gun. Although in 1867 the government bought fifty Gatling guns caliber .50, and fifty caliber 1.00, the first for fifteen hundred dollars and the second for a thousand dollars each, in 1862 the government also bought some fifty Union Repeating Guns, pieces consisting of two rifled barrels which operated in front of a breech mechanism. President Lincoln nicknamed them the "coffeymills." Thus the machine gun was not used extensively during the Civil War.

The machine gun attracted more attention in Europe. In Belgium, around 1851, there originated the Montigny Mitrailleuse (named from the French *mitraille,* which means "grapeshot"). Even though it was subsequently improved, the Montigny Mitrailleuse always remained a heavy, clumsy weapon mounted on a wheeled carriage and horse drawn, much like a piece of light artillery, which it resembled. It consisted of many barrels, as many as thirty. Perforated iron plates holding the cartridges were fitted into the grooves of the breechblock which forced the cartridges into their respective chambers when it was locked. The barrels fired successively when the gunner turned a crank.

Napoleon III was so impressed with the performance of the Mitrailleuse that he ordered his army to adopt it on the eve of the Franco-Prussian War of 1870. Because it sent a hail of bullets like grapeshot, because it was mounted and horse drawn, the French Army classified the weapon as artillery and, consequently, reorganized its light artillery groups. Whereas the group had consisted of three batteries, each composed of six guns, the new arrangement provided for only two gun batteries, the third being replaced by ten machine guns. The French made a great mistake; they misunderstood the mission of the new weapon. Its short range as well as its hitting power were those of the rifle. It merely multiplied the rifle's effect, giving its gunner a fire capacity equal to that of many infantrymen. When used at extreme range as an auxiliary to the field gun it was worthless. Every French artillery group that met a similar unit of the Prussian Army was thus handicapped by the defection of one battery. The inferiority of the French artillery was one of the causes leading to utter defeat.

The Mitrailleuse was used more successfully to support the infantry. Yet its clumsy carriage was visible from a long distance. Whenever the Prussians encountered a position defended by a conspicuous Mitrailleuse they held back their infantry beyond the weapon's short range and brought up a light fieldpiece to knock it out of action. Thus the machine gun made a poor showing in a war that was a major test of its effectiveness. The misunderstanding by the French of the use to which it was destined considerably retarded the progress of the weapon as a tool of warfare.

The Gatling gun, inasmuch as it was not so subject to stoppages, was superior to the Montigny Mitrailleuse. Russia appreciated the difference when she adopted the gun extensively, and the Gatling gun met success as the Russians' main defensive weapon to cover lines of approach during the Russo-Turkish War of 1877. Other models appeared in the United States, where the metallic cartridge offered a better chance. The Lowell machine gun, for instance, had only three revolving barrels. The Gardner had four rifled barrels and was operated by turning a drum-shaped instrument mounted on a transverse axis in the rear of the barrels. The turning of the crank prevented accurate firing. The pieces were mounted on a wheeled carriage, a fact which checked the progress of the weapon.

In 1883 the first sound machine gun in which the operations of extracting, ejecting, feeding, and firing were performed automatically was invented by Hiram S. Maxim. The engineer was born at Brockway's Mills, Maine, on February 5, 1840. In 1880 he went over to England with his invention and became an English subject. He merged with the Nordenfelt Company in 1888 and in 1896 he was absorbed into the Vickers Sons and Maxim Company, a firm which became known as Vickers Ltd., after 1911. Maxim died on November 24, 1916. His invention was a true one and all the devices which we use now are based on the same principles.

Maxim's rapid-fire gun consisted of a single barrel; it was self-loading and fired upon one squeeze of the trigger. The source of energy which the inventor used to perform the automatic operation was the force of recoil —indirectly, the expansive power of the propelling gases in the chamber. Maxim got the idea to use the force of recoil when one day the heavy impact of a high caliber gun which he had just fired bruised his right shoulder. He used the power to move the breechbolt backward, thus extracting and ejecting the empty case. When the breechbolt again moved forward, pushing a fresh cartridge into the chamber, the gun was then cocked and ready to fire the next round. By keeping the trigger depressed the cycle of fire was continuous until stopped by either expending the belt of ammunition or releasing the trigger.

The Maxim machine gun fired the standard small-arms metallic cartridges which were fed by means of a belt sliding transversely at the breech. The reader knows that when a shot is fired the explosion produces heat, some of which is transferred to the steel barrel. Now in a single-shot rifle the barrel absorbs the heat or cools off before the operator has a chance to fire again. However, where a machine gun intended for rapid and sustained fire is concerned the effects are cumulative. In other words, each additional shot increases the temperature of the barrel which, as the heat rises, becomes more malleable and sensitive to the friction of bullets. Should a soldier fire a noncooled gun for five minutes without stopping, upon examining the barrel he would find that

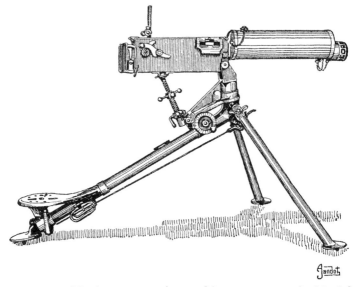

FIGURE 17. *Maxim automatic machine gun, .30 cal., Model 1904.*

its bore had lost all traces of rifling. Thus some measure has to be taken to cool the barrel. Maxim decided to do this by surrounding it with a steel jacket containing cold water. As the water begins to boil after 6,000 rounds of sustained fire, two portholes on the top of the jacket provide exit for the steam. Whenever the barrel is slanted, a sleeve valve operating by gravity slides over the port-hole which would ordinarily allow the water to escape. The water is usually replaced every 2,000 rounds. When freezing weather is anticipated while the machine gun awaits for action, the operator usually lowers the water's freezing point by adding glycerin, alcohol, or even common salt.

Maxim's gun was heavy and was at first mounted on wheels. Furnished later on with a tripod, it was lightened sufficiently for two men to carry it. Even though some military leaders considered the weapon too complicated for the battlefield and experts maintained that it would be impossible to supply the necessary cartridges to feed this ammunition-greedy machine, the Maxim's rate of fire (approximately four hundred shots per minute) and its mechanical efficiency induced the British Army to adopt the weapon officially in 1891. Germany, which still uses the Maxims, did not issue machine guns to its army before 1895.

In 1895, John M. Browning found a new method, an invention in its own right, of securing energy to perform the automatic steps of extracting, ejecting, feeding, and firing. Instead of using the recoil force, which after all was an indirect way of employing the expansive force of the propelling gases, Browning diverted a slight part of the hot gases to do the work. In one of the grooves inside the barrel's bore, near the muzzle, the inventor drilled a microscopic porthole, not large enough to interfere with the bullet's passage. The porthole communicated with an auxiliary cylinder situated under the barrel and housing a piston. As the propellent gases forced the bullet over the porthole, a slight portion of the expanding gases escaped into the auxiliary cylinder, forcing the piston backward. The piston, in turn, tilted a lever and set in motion the breech mechanism to extract and eject the empty case and to reload and fire a fresh cartridge. This type of mechanism, entirely the

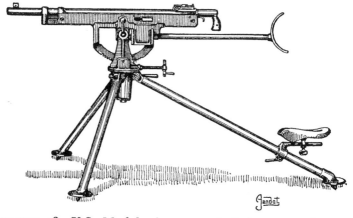

FIGURE 18. *U.S. Model 1895, .30-cal. Colt automatic machine gun.*

invention of Browning, is known as "gas-operated," while the other system is Maxim's "recoil-operated." The latter is favored for heavy machine guns, from which a sustained, accurate fire is expected. That the Browning system was efficient for lighter guns is shown by the fact that it is now used on our new Garand rifle.

Browning's invention of 1895 was first manufactured by the Colt's Patent Fire Arms Manufacturing Company, Hartford, Connecticut. In addition to being gas-operated, it was also air-cooled—to nullify the tremendous heat generated by sustained fire, which can so increase the barrel's diameter that the bullet no longer fits the bore, thus causing gas leakage and making the grooves useless. This heat is not counteracted by any other means than by exposing the barrel's surface to the air. Browning placed flanges around the barrel, to dissipate more readily the heat. The Colt machine gun, as it is now called, was used in the Spanish-American War.

In their war in South Africa the British also used a Maxim machine gun of caliber 1.457 inch (37mm.), firing explosive shells weighing one pound. Called the "Pom-Pom," it was not capable of very rapid fire and its success was limited. Yet it is interesting to see that the question of using machine guns of caliber .50 or even heavier (such as the 20-mm. Oerlikon aircraft cannon manufactured today) preceded the arrival of planes and tanks as major tactical factors.

The Russo-Japanese War provided the first large-scale test of the machine gun. The Russians were at first armed with a Maxim mounted on wheels, but they soon adopted a tripod. The Japanese had the Hotchkiss (8mm.), an air-cooled, gas-operated machine invented by an Austrian, Captain von Odkolek, in 1897. Both the Russians and the Japanese used the weapon with great success, at times wiping out whole battalions.

When we entered the first World War machine guns were used defensively (cross fire) and offensively (overhead fire). For both uses the heavy machine gun was preferable. However, it could not keep up with the movement of infantry and a light shoulder piece was adopted to give support and firing power to small infantry groups. The Allies followed two systems of fighting with machine guns. The French employed the heavy machine gun (Hotchkiss, 8mm.) and the automatic rifle (Chauchat). The English supplemented the heavy Vickers and their Hotchkiss automatic rifle (known as the Benet-Mercié in this country) with the Lewis light machine gun of intermediate weight. Since our government decided that the Army should co-operate with the French, it was desirable that we should follow their method of using the machine gun.

We entered the war with only a few machine guns. We had in stock some of the Colt guns with which we had fought the Spanish-American War. These gas-operated, air-cooled guns, firing 450 shots per minute, were by no means outmoded, some having been ordered by the Allies. Yet early in 1917 we stopped production of the type and used what we had for training purposes. We also had a few Benet-Mercié automatic rifles, a type invented about 1900 by the American Lawrence Benet. We had adopted it around 1909, as had also the British, who called it the light Hotchkiss after the name of the original manufacturer. Because it weighed too much (30 pounds) for an automatic rifle designed to be operated by one man, and because it was too complicated, the United States discarded the weapon in 1914. Thus, even though we had the heavy Colt and the Benet-Mercié machine rifle, we did not have either in sufficient quantities to satisfy the needs of our growing field forces. Therefore, at the beginning of the struggle we had to use the Hotchkiss and the Chauchat until the weapons which we had adopted to replace the Colt and the Benet-Mercié were obtainable. The Hotchkiss heavy machine gun, the standard French weapon manufactured by the Hotchkiss Company, St. Étienne, France, was used widely on the Western Front. It fired the 8-mm. (.31-inch) Lebel ammunition. The Chauchat automatic rifle, Model 1915, was used extensively by our expeditionary

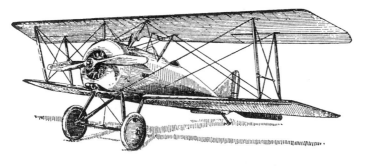

FIGURE 19. *A 1918 model Thomas-Morse pursuit plane.*

forces; it was a recoil-operated, air-cooled weapon, firing the Lebel (8-mm.) ammunition, three hundred shots per minute. Weighing only 19 pounds, this gun could be fired from either the shoulder or the hip. Supported by a bipod, it was fed by means of a semicircular clip holding twenty cartridges and attached under the barrel.

The United States Army also used the Berthier light machine gun, caliber .30 (U.S. service ammunition, Model 1906). The invention of a Frenchman, General Berthier, it was gas-operated, air-cooled, and fired six hundred shots per minute. Since it weighed only 15 pounds, this type could be fired with the aid of a bipod or from the hip and shoulder. Although this remarkable weapon was perfected in the United States, we did not have the manufacturing facilities to produce it in large quantities.

In 1917 the Savage Arms Corporation, Utica, New York, was manufacturing the Lewis machine gun for the British Government. Invented in 1896 by Col. I. N. Lewis, United States Coast Artillery, retired, this gun had been adopted by the British Army. The United States ordered some of the Lewis guns to be manufactured to use our .30-caliber service ammunition. The gun was issued to the United States Marine Corps and was used for training purposes in the Army. Gas-operated and air-cooled, it fired six hundred shots per minute. An aluminum radiator surrounded the barrel and drew the gases which cleared the muzzle, thus creating a draft that absorbed the heat. The gun weighed 36 pounds and could be fired from a bipod and from the hip or shoulder; it was fed by a circular magazine holding forty-seven rounds. The Lewis machine gun was also modified for service as an aircraft weapon. The modifications consisted in replacing the regular shoulder stock with a spade grip, removing the radiator, and adding special sights that accounted for the motion of both the firer and his target. No special cooling agent is needed in an aircraft machine gun, for the temperature is lower at high altitudes and the speed of the craft provides a good draft.

The United States developed another aircraft machine gun in 1917: the Marlin gun. Really an adaptation of the Colt gun, it was a gas-operated, air-cooled piece firing six hundred and eighty rounds per minute of the .30-caliber service ammunition and also adoptable for the synchronizing attachment. When a pursuit plane fires, its gun is aimed by pointing the plane's nose toward the target. Thus, when a machine gun has to fire through the propeller, a device has to be used to

FIGURE 20. *Vickers synchronized machine guns on SPAD XIII plane, 1918.*

synchronize the rate and time of fire with the movement of the propeller so that the bullets may pass when the blades are away; otherwise the propeller's blades would be torn into shreds. The Marlin machine gun was used also in tanks.

The Vickers machine gun, England's Maxim type, was also manufactured here and used for aircraft work. A Vickers 11-mm. gun, caliber .43, was also mounted on airplanes. Most of these aircraft machine guns were fed by what is called a metallic disintegrating feed belt.

This consists of metallic links connected by the cartridges. When the cartridge is fed into the chamber the link is disconnected and dropped outside the craft. This method, although more expensive, was adopted because an aircraft gunner had no assistant to rearrange an emptied feed belt.

Soon after our entry in the first World War the United States Army selected the Browning heavy machine gun

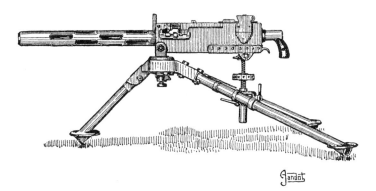

Gandot

FIGURE 21. *U.S. machine gun, .30 cal., Browning Model 1919A4 mounted on M2 ground mount. (Air cooled.)*

and the Browning automatic rifle as its standard weapons. It had only used the Hotchkiss, Benet-Mercié, and Chauchat because the Brownings were not yet obtainable. But it was not until June, 1918, that production of both assumed large-scale proportions. Firing and endurance tests proved that the two Brownings were superior to any weapon being used by the Allies or the Germans. The Browning heavy machine gun M1917A1, caliber .30, using service ammunition Model 1906, is of the recoil-operated, water-cooled type, firing five hundred shots per minute. It was invented by John M. Browning and manufactured by Colt's Patent Fire Arms Manufacturing Company of Hartford, Connecticut. It is fed by means of a webbing belt holding two hundred and fifty rounds. When the water jacket is full the gun weighs over 36 pounds, and the tripod upon which it is mounted averages 50 pounds. The gun was manufactured in quantity and is still our official weapon: we have about seventy thousand such pieces either issued to the troops or in stores. Even though it was manufactured during the first World War, this machine gun is by no means obsolete, nor will it be for some time to come, for the German and British Armies still fight with Maxims and Vickers respectively, both of which are older models. There has been a trend in the United States recently to modernize the Browning by removing the water jacket and replacing it with an air-cooled, skeletonized steel tube. It is this new type which is being mounted upon our tanks and armored cars. New tactics no longer make it desirable to lay machine-gun barrages maintained by continuous fire; the present stress is upon short, intensified bursts which do not heat the barrel sufficiently to make water cooling necessary. Moreover, the need for maintaining a water supply, in addition to the clumsiness of the water jacket, makes water cooling inadvisable for the tanks and armored cars.

The Browning automatic rifle M1918, caliber .30, invented by the same man and manufactured by the same company, is fired from either the shoulder or from the hip. It is a gas-operated, air-cooled weapon, carried by means of a sling similar to that of the service rifle. The gun weighs only 15.5 pounds, has a length of 47 inches, and is fed by means of a clip holding twenty cartridges.

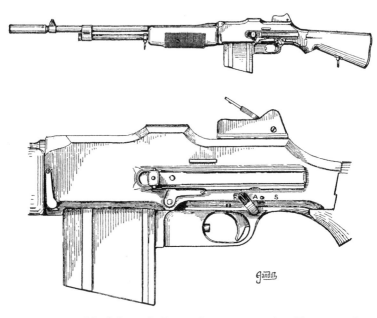

FIGURE 22. *Model 1918, Browning automatic rifle, .30 cal., and close-up of Browning action.*

It fires the standard service ammunition. Although it was not designed for sustained fire, it can deliver six hundred shots per minute. One important fact about the weapon is that it can fire semiautomatically—one single shot for each squeeze of the trigger—whenever the operator turns a change lever. The semiautomatic firing, about sixty shots per minute, is more accurate than the rapid automatic fire, for, as the reader will remember, the cumulating effects of recoil force the light gun's muzzle upward during continued firing. It is principally for this reason that the automatic rifle is not suited for overhead fire (against airplanes) or against any distant target that requires accuracy rather than volume. The defect does not apply to the Browning automatic rifle in particular but to all such light weapons intended to deliver large volumes of fire. As a matter of fact, the Browning, because of its lightness, simplicity, maneuverability, and ballistic powers, is probably the best weapon of its kind. We have large quantities on hand and one automatic is issued to each rifle squad of the infantry. The Browning automatic and the new Garand semiautomatic ought to furnish our infantry units with a volume of fire equaled by no other army.

The advent of airplanes forced the United States to adopt the Browning aircraft machine gun M1918A2, caliber .30, using the service ammunition. It is recoil-operated and air-cooled by means of a skeletonized steel tube which replaces the water jacket of the Browning. Its maximum rate of fire is twelve hundred and fifty shots per minute, a large volume made necessary by the fleeting character of aircraft targets. An aircraft gunner will catch his enemy in his sights for a split second, and it is urgent that he should deliver as intense a burst of bullets as possible. In our modern pursuit planes three of these guns are located inside each wing; the British Hurricane even has four, making a total of eight machine guns. In aircraft, synchronized machine guns, the rate of fire is twelve hundred shots per minute. The planes usually go up with a 15-second supply of ammunition per gun to be fired in bursts lasting from one to three seconds. Although the piece can be used with a synchronizer to fire through the propeller blades, the

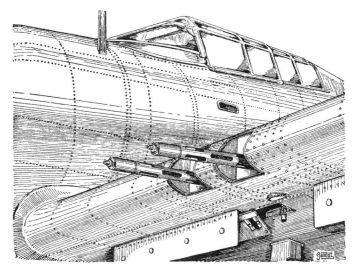

FIGURE 23. *Machine guns (.30 cal., M2) mounted in the wing of an XP43 plane (1941).*

Ordnance Department only furnishes the gun; it has nothing to do either with synchronizing or feeding devices, which come under the Air Corps. A .50-caliber, air-cooled type has been developed for use in aircrafts and tanks as has also a water-cooled model for use as an antiaircraft weapon.

The changes in tactics affecting the use of the machine gun have also influenced the type of ammunition desired. Fresh from the lessons taught by the first World War, which was a war of position rather than of movement, one extolling defensive rather than offensive warfare, we set about looking for a cartridge that would give

FIGURE 24. *A modern Curtiss O-1-G Falcon fighter with a 425-h.p., 12-cylinder motor.*

us the long range needed for defensive machine-gun barrages. Thus, in 1926, we adopted the M-1, boat-tailed (172 grains) type of bullet, with a maximum range of 5,500 yards and ballistic qualities making it suitable for machine-gun barrages. In the thirties, however, because our National Guard ranges did not allow the firing with safety of the M-1 cartridge and because altered tactics no longer call for machine-gun barrages and extreme ranges, we adopted the M-2 (flat-base, 152-grain bullet) type of cartridge. In spite of the growing use of machine guns and automatic weapons, in spite of the firing power of airplanes, tanks, and of the rifle squad, the Army does not anticipate a small-arms ammunition shortage, not even in the event of war. In addition to our vast stores, we have a monthly output of one hundred million .45-caliber (pistol), .30-caliber, and .50-

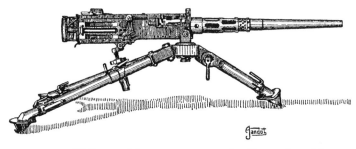

FIGURE 25. *U.S. machine gun, .50 cal., Browning M2 on mount M3. (Heavy barrel, air cooled.)*

caliber ammunition. Within six months this monthly production will have increased to two hundred and fifty millions.

The development of the machine gun was a great step in the progress of weapons. It revolutionized tactics, brought forth new war monsters, and helped to stabilize warfare. Soldiers accustomed to the triumphal march, to the sweeping war of movement had to seek cover. The machine gun was the main weapon responsible for the defensive character of the first World War. Barrages proved so effective that a sortie from a trench often meant suicide. Grenades and mortars were powerless against the extreme range of the machine gun. The war had almost reached an unhealthy stalemate when the British conceived the idea of a moving, armored vehicle —the tank—as a means of pitting machine gun against machine gun and dealing with the machine gun nest. Thus the tank and even the plane, both of which play such an important part in the tactics of the present war, owe their success to a large extent to the firing power that the machine gun affords them.

CHAPTER FIVE

GRENADES AND MORTARS

UNLIKE THE machine gun, the grenade (named after the pomegranate, Latin, *granatum*) is an ancient weapon. It was used as early as the fifteenth century and was widely employed during the seventeenth. Vauban, the famous French military engineer, used about twenty thousand in his siege of Namur in 1692. The grenade of those days weighed about 2½ pounds and consisted of a hollow, cast-iron ball filled with black powder and furnished with a fuse. The soldier ignited the fuse with a slow match, whirled the missile around to spur the lighted fuse, and tossed the grenade at the enemy. The primitive grenades were so treacherous that they often exploded in the thrower's hand or burst sufficiently close to him to inflict wounds. Therefore the soldiers who risked their lives to throw grenades were men of unusual courage and physical strength. With the increasing use of the weapon, the grenadiers began to form battalions and regiments, establishing a tradition. For long after grenades had disappeared, the Grenadiers, brave and handsome, were still the pride of their country.

The improvement of firearms at the beginning of the eighteenth century spelled the obliteration of the grenade. The weapon was not used, not even during Napoleon's campaigns, until the American Civil War. In

this conflict hand bombs in 1-, 3-, and 5-pound sizes, manufactured in New York City on East Twenty-third Street
and provided with a percussion cap, were used for combat at close quarters. But grenades were not used again
to any extent until the Russo-Japanese War. The conditions at the siege of Port Arthur necessitated the use
of the weapon for fighting at close range. The Russians
improvised grenades by filling empty artillery cases or
shells with guncotton and fitting a certain length of
safety fuse. As a result of the Russo-Japanese War most
nations experimented with the reborn weapon, but
when the first World War settled down to trench warfare the Germans alone were well equipped with grenades. The type generally adopted was one resembling a
potato masher, the explosive sphere or cylinder being
fitted with a wooden handle sometimes as long as 15
inches. When the soldier hurled the grenade from
within a narrow trench he often hit the rear wall with
the weapon, which burst, crippling him. When the
United States entered the war, our Army had the experience of the Allies to guide its adoption of suitable
weapons.

Grenades are generally divided according to their
usage into five classes: (1) the defensive grenade; (2) the offensive grenade; (3) the gas grenade; (4) the phosphorous
grenade; and (5) the incendiary grenade. Our defensive
hand grenade, Mark II, is similar to the famous Mills grenade used by the British. It is approximately the size of a
large lemon, and its cast-iron body bears deep vertical
and horizontal furrows which divide the surface into
fragments. Thus the common appellation "40-fragmen-

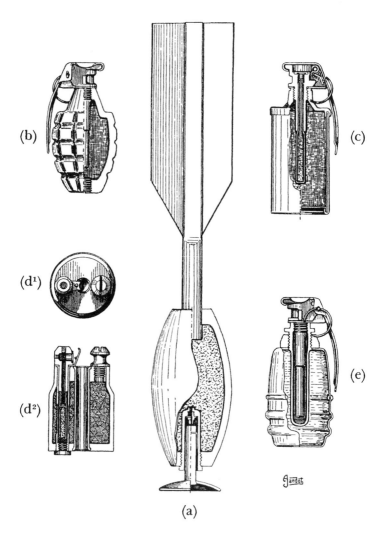

FIGURE 26. *Hand Grenades.* (a) *Civil War percussion hand grenade;* (b) *defensive Mark II fragmental hand grenade;* (c) *offensive Mark III hand grenade;* (d¹) *and* (d²) *V-B rifle grenade;* (e) *gas grenade Mark V.*

tation" came into use because the grenade is divided roughly into forty pieces. This body is filled with an explosive charge, namely, 2⅓ ounces of Trojan powder. Trojan powder is a dry explosive consisting of four parts of nitrostarch (purified starch dipped into a mixture of nitric and sulphuric acids and washed) and of six parts of ammonium and sodium nitrates. Into the upper extremity of the body is screwed the bouchon assembly, which consists of the bouchon, the operating lever, and the sheet steel sealer. The bouchon itself is a die casting composed of a tube housing the standard Bickford safety fuse and leading to a fulminated detonator situated in the center of the explosive charge. The head of the bouchon remaining outside the body holds the priming cap, the firing spring, and the striker. A safety pin with a ring attached to it holds in place the operating lever which fits over the bouchon's head. There exists also a dummy grenade, now used for practice instead of the black-powder charge previously employed. It consists of a cast-iron body similar to that of the defensive grenade with the single exception that it is painted red in contrast to the gray of live grenades.

To use the grenade, the soldier holds it in his right hand, placing his fingers over the operating lever. He then removes the safety pin by pulling the ring and hurls the missile toward the target. When the operating lever is freed from the thrower's grip, the firing spring activates a pin which ejects the lever and forces the striker against a priming cap. The fuse is ignited and, after about five seconds, the detonator explodes, causing the main charge to burst violently. The cast-iron body breaks into fragments, many of which fly upward and some of which are propelled to distances as great as 100 feet. These fragments lose their velocity and effectiveness rapidly. A man standing within 15 or 20 yards of the explosion may receive severe wounds, and he will not escape injuries at a distance of 10 yards unless he is in a prone position. Fragments, however, may be thrown to a much greater distance, and the thrower, who has an average range of 40 yards, should never hurl a grenade unless he is under cover. Because of its highly curved trajectory, a grenade can reach a trench, a hole, a dugout, or any protected position hidden from the thrower by either a wall, a ridge, or some natural obstacle. Thus the defensive grenade, because of its wide radius of effectiveness, is particularly useful in dispersing an attacking force. The grenade is not an integral part of a soldier's equipment, and it is only distributed when the circumstances demand it. Since the present war is one of movement, there is only limited use of the grenade, which is particularly designed for siege and trench warfare.

The offensive hand grenade, Mark III, consists of a cardboard cylindrical body topped by a die-cast cone threaded to receive the same bouchon assembly as the one used in the defensive grenade. It operates in a similar fashion. The grenade explodes with extreme violence. Yet a soldier in the open, rushing to the attack, can hurl it at his enemy with relative safety, since the lack of fragmentation or cast-iron parts (except for the bouchon which constitutes the most danger) limits the effectiveness of the blast to 15 yards. The phosphorous hand grenade, Mark II, consists of a barrel-like steel container 3½ inches high and 2¼ inches in diameter, into the center of which a steel thimble is screwed to house the bouchon and separate its fuse and detonator from the phosphorous charge in the body. Upon explosion, the phosphorous is set free and reacts with the air to burn and form a foglike gas which disperses to a radius of 10 yards. This grenade is used, therefore, to screen small movements. The gas is similar in form to the phosphorous grenade except that its body is surrounded near the bottom by two annular corrugations to distinguish it. It is charged with stannic tetrachloride, a lachrymator or tear-producing gas employed in subduing mobs and quieting riots. The incendiary grenade, the body of which is filled with solid oil and thermit, operates in the same manner.

The rifle grenade, which has a maximum range of 300 yards, is the intermediate weapon between the hand grenade and the light trench mortar. In 1917 we adopted the type invented by two Frenchmen, Viven and Bessière. It is in their honor that the weapon is called the V.B. rifle grenade. Its length is 2½ inches, its diameter 2 inches, and it is fired from a funnel-like discharger which is attached to the muzzle of the service rifle. The body is a cylinder of malleable iron grooved on the inside so that it will fragment upon explosion. The base is flat and a lengthwise tube passes through the cylinder's center. It is through this tube that the bullet travels when the regular cartridge is fired. The striker projects obliquely over the end of the tube so that when the bullet goes through the tube it hits the striker which, in turn, fires the primer. The flash is caught by the fuse, travels down for eight seconds, and sets off the detonator. The detonator tube bursts and the main charge explodes. All these operations are carried out while the grenade rushes to its target, for it begins to travel as soon as the bullet enters its central tube. When the grenade leaves the discharger—a steel cylinder tapering at one end to fit over the muzzle—the bullet is not the propellant, but rather the gases behind the bullet, which exert pressure upon the grenade's flat base in the tromblon or discharger. The rifle grenades proved very satisfactory during the first World War, but the weight and bulkiness of its ammunition limited the use of the weapon. During the last war and up to 1930, we also employed the rod grenade, which was fired from a rifle by means of a blank cartridge.

Light trench mortars, along with hand and rifle grenades, constitute the artillery belonging to the common infantry regiment. The trench mortar is a relatively new weapon ushered in by World War I. Previous to our entry in the war the United States Army had only experimented with a 3.2-inch type which had never seen active service. Moreover, the Allies had not placed any orders for trench mortars in this country and no manufacturing facilities were available. The Ordnance Department had to start from the very beginning. We finally adopted the 3-inch Stokes type used by the British.

The trench mortar consists of a barrel weighing 43 pounds, of a mounting weighing 37 pounds, and of a base plate weighing 28 pounds. The barrel is a smoothbore, solid steel tube, with an anvil pillar or firing pin at the base. The mounting consists of a trunnion which grasps the barrel and establishes the range by sliding up and down between the two legs of the bipod. The steel base plate holds the tube down. The three parts—tube, mounting, and base plate—can be transported separately by hand to the front line and assembled for firing. The

FIGURE 27. *U.S. mortar 81-mm. M1.*

shell consists of an iron tubing case filled with the explosive charge. At one end there are the percussion fuse and the detonator to set off the main charge when the shell falls to the ground. At the other, at the base, a smaller tube is attached into which a blank shotgun cartridge is inserted to propel the shell, which weighs 12 pounds. If a range exceeding 300 yards is desired, a few rings of ballistite explosive are placed around the cartridge.

To fire the weapon, the operator inserts the blank cartridge into the smaller tube and drops the shell into the barrel through the muzzle. The shell slides down and the blank cartridge hits the anvil pillar, thus exploding and propelling the shell out of the barrel. The range can be regulated to vary from 100 to 800 yards and the normal rate of fire is ten rounds per minute. Although the mortar is not as accurate as it might be, this inaccuracy is more than made up by an effective radius of 30 yards. The muzzle velocity of the projectile is low, but its curved trajectory and high angle of fire are the characteristics that make the weapon effective. It can be fired from any defiladed position, such as a trench or shell hole, and fire can be directed against troop concentrations or machine-gun nests protected by natural barriers like a ridge. The terrific burst of its high-explosive shell has a shattering effect upon morale.

The United States Army has recently adopted an improved trench mortar, known as the Stokes-Brandt M1. Although it is similar to the Stokes, it is provided with elaborate sighting and laying instruments, and the projectile does not tumble in its course. The shells used are of two types: one weighs 14 pounds and has a maximum range of 1,300 yards, while the second weighs only 7½ pounds and has a maximum range of 3,250 yards. The gun barrel weighs 44½ pounds and the total weight is 91½ pounds. A smaller weapon was also adopted, the 60-mm. trench mortar M2, with a total weight of 27¼ pounds. The infantry regiment of an armored division has eight Stokes-Brandt (81mm.), each one transported on a half-track carrier and attended by a squad of seven men armed with pistols. In addition, the regiment has eighteen trench mortars (60mm.). Each is attended by a squad of five men armed with pistols. The corporal of the squad carries the base plate, the Number 1 man has the tube and the tripod, and the three other men carry bags of ammunition.

Of course, heavier trench mortars are used. Yet they are classified as field artillery and are not part of the armament which the infantry carries into the field. With the light trench mortar, we come to the last weapon which belongs to the infantry as part of its regular equipment.

CHAPTER SIX

FIELD ARTILLERY

AUTHORITIES generally accept 1250 as the approximate date upon which the cannon (from Latin *canna,* "tube") made its appearance. Thus the cannon has evolutionized over a period of almost seven centuries, from the most primitive gun tube to our new 16-inch guns. This development can be divided into three phases or epochs. The first, ending around 1520, is characterized by the use of the stoneshot. The gun tubes themselves were generally made of wrought iron, which was stronger and less expensive than bronze. The second period begins with the use of cast-iron spherical shot, of bronze and cast-iron guns, of corn powder instead of serpentine powder, and it extends until 1852. The third or new epoch starts in 1852 and extends to the present. It is a period of great achievements, including the employment of rifling, the use of elongated projectiles, the invention of smokeless powder, the improvement of steel, and many other steps which open new horizons for the future of gunmaking.

As early as 1338 both iron and brass (a very crude alloy of copper and zinc) cannons of small caliber were used widely in Europe. Their missiles at first were arrows, but they gradually employed stones, as spherical as possible. The propellant was black powder, or rather "serpentine," a rough, heterogeneous mixture of saltpeter, sul-

phur, and charcoal named after the small guns in which
it was first used. The light guns were strapped to heavy
wooden beams called cradles. During the fourteenth and
fifteenth centuries states eagerly built huge cannons capable of throwing stones sufficiently heavy to dent and
break the pachydermous walls of medieval castles. However, these guns will be treated as heavy artillery in the

FIGURE 28. *Bronze cannon. Circa 1500–1600.*

next chapter. In order to defend the fortifications, a
"wall" gun was devised consisting of a small-caliber,
wrought-iron tube supported by a metal fork, the handle
of which was driven into the wall. The tube was held to
the fork by means of a wrought-iron trunnion, composed
of two short arms projecting at right angles from the
tube's sides. The wall cannon was provided with a number of removable breechblocks so that one could be inserted and fired while the others were loaded. There were
other attempts at breech-loading, but, until 1850, they

all proved impractical and even dangerous. The breech was naturally weakened and the gun easily burst. Besides, the poor workmanship made obturation, the sealing of gases behind the projectile, by means of a breechblock impossible. Muzzle-loading cannons remained supreme.

At the beginning of the fifteenth century Europeans had small muzzle-loading mortars cast in bronze integral with the base at an elevation of 45 degrees. It was not until the next century, however, that the art of casting metals and of finding additional supplies permitted the use of metal projectiles. These projectiles, concentrating more weight into less volume, wrought greater destruction than the stone missiles of the heavy cannons (bombards) which gave way to guns with an average caliber of 5 inches. Most of the guns were held to their heavy wooden cradle by means of a trunnion and were mounted on wheels for greater mobility. Although the use of corn powder in cannons was banned at first because it was too powerful for the crudely constructed tubes, it soon supplanted serpentine powder. The principles of rifling discovered in the sixteenth century were not followed to their practical conclusion for nearly three hundred years, notwithstanding some experimental but unsuccessful types tried in England in 1745—breech-loading, rifled cannons with the breech opening at the side.

During the seventeenth and eighteenth centuries a distrust of cast-iron and steel guns arose among soldiers and manufacturers. Because the materials used were poor and the manufacturing processes were still primitive, many cannon tubes burst. Bronze guns, therefore, were generally favored and constituted a large part of the artillery which General Washington employed in the American Revolutionary War. Cannons were then cast with a core, that is, a shaft of iron covered with clay was inserted into the mold to secure the bore. In spite of special care and arrangement, either the frame, mold, or shaft moved when the molten metal was poured into the mold so that the bore was never precise, straight, or even parallel to the axis of the cast. Moreover, under the heat of the metal the core would often warp or air bubbles would remain imprisoned when the cast cooled off. In order to avoid such defects, Moritz of Geneva introduced the boring of cannons from a solid piece of iron in 1739. The method was adopted widely, and it was soon discovered that a more exact bore would result if the gun tube instead of the drill revolved through horse or water power, or if one bore-size drill were employed instead of a number of drills graduating in size.

There was also a tendency around that time to standardize the calibers of cannons and their carriages. The two French chiefs of artillery between 1750 and 1780, de Vallière and Gribeauval, were particularly important in the work of standardization carried on throughout Europe. Moreover, the balk of timber or the trail was lengthened and so fashioned that it might be fastened to the ground to prevent recoil. Gribeauval, around 1865, replaced the hardwood axle—which supported the wheels and the trail—by an iron axle. A wooden arc was also fixed to the trail near the breech, which gave the desired elevation by moving up and down. Although standardization was not important from the point of view of technical improvement, it showed the part which artillery was to play in military affairs.

As late as 1600 guns were not provided with any means for sighting. Their maximum effective range of 100 yards did not allow the target to be so distant that any method other than pointing the gun in a general direction was

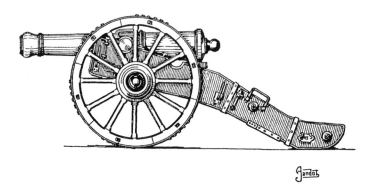

FIGURE 29. *Model 1750 field gun. Gribeauval type (French).*

necessary. When the use of corn powder and metal projectiles increased the range, gunmakers provided their products with "dispart" sights. These consisted of two notches, one fore sight up on the muzzle ring and the other upon the breech, both elevated to such an extent that an imaginary line connecting them would have been parallel to the axis of the tube. This type was well suited for short ranges where direction was the only problem. Gunners realized, however, that as long as the powder charge and the projectile remained constant a degree of elevation would be needed to secure additional distance. Around 1775, to solve the problem, Gribeauval introduced the tangent sight, a brass rule graduated into divisions corresponding to the tangents of angles and provided with a metal slide to permit the gunner to lay his piece both in elevation and in direction. Such tangent scales were used widely by the United States Army before 1812.

With the exception of the mortars, all the guns were more or less horizontally fired, a fire only effective on relatively level terrains. To reach targets hidden behind ridges or fortifications, gunners needed a high-angle fire. Thus the howitzer (German *haubitze* from Czech *houfnice,* meaning a "catapult") was introduced in the French Army in 1785. During the French Revolution, when the French Army was faced by hostile armies at the frontiers, it decided to adopt horse artillery. The resulting mobility multiplied the effects of French artillery, allowing it to co-operate with the infantry and to follow it in action. The multiplied power of her artillery and the co-operation between the artillery and the infantry saved France from defeat. Napoleon realized the importance of artillery perhaps more than any other preceding military leader and made full use of it in his tactics. In 1800, to increase its mobility, he paired off the horses and placed a rider on each horse, as is still done today in the United States Army, where prime movers or self-propelled mounts have not yet supplanted the horse artillery.

Little progress was made in the early part of the nineteenth century. The advantage of rifling field guns was recognized, but, as in the case of the rifle, it was looked upon as impractical. If the rifled gun was a muzzle-loader,

it became that much more difficult to load, for the projectile had to fit the bore very tightly. Thus a breech-
loading system was the only answer. Another problem
was whether the elongated projectile should supplant
the spherical type. Different trials took place in Europe.
Most of the models were muzzle-loading rifled guns. All
the attempts at introducing the rifled guns failed because
the pieces were too difficult to load. In 1845, however,
Major Cavalli of Sardinia brought out a rifled gun with
the wedge type of breechblock. About the same time
Baron Wahrendorff of Sweden introduced a similar system of breech-loading. The elongated projectile replaced
the spherical type; it was inserted into the chamber
through the breech opening. From a practical point of
view, the Wahrendorff and Cavalli systems were not as
successful as they might have been, for the guns were
made of cast iron, which was so weak that the breech
usually gave way after a few rounds. There was also another defect. It was impossible to secure any satisfying
degree of obturation, that is, to prevent the escape of gases
through the breech opening. It was of the utmost importance to obtain obturation if the power propelling the
missile were not to be reduced. In spite of the faults involved in the systems, breech-loading and rifling were
here to stay.

The subject of rifling was sponsored effectively in
France by Colonel Treuille de Beaulieu from 1840 till
1852. At that time Louis Napoleon staged his famous
coup d'état and crowned himself emperor. This advent to
power was a good omen for the new artillery, for the emperor was something of an authority on artillery, its his-

tory and its problems. He lent a willing ear to Treuille de Beaulieu, and in 1854, during the Crimean War, when the French troops with their short-range, smooth-bore cannons made no headway in their siege of Sebastopol, Napoleon III ordered that intensive experiments be carried out with the new system. Some brass guns were rifled and sent first to Algeria and then to Cochin China for trials. The great test for the new artillery took place during Napoleon III's campaign in Italy in 1856 when French artillery firing from well-protected positions in the rear crushed the charges of Austrian cavalry and demoralized the infantry with case shot and canister.

As a result of this success, most European countries quickly adopted the system of rifling and breech-loading. Only England persisted in keeping rifled muzzle-loaders as late as 1880. It was around 1850 that the Englishman Sir William Armstrong left the legal profession to apply himself to engineering. He perfected the manufacture of both muzzle-loading and breech-loading rifled guns. He realized that cast iron, no matter how well prepared, would always burst, even with a moderate charge of black powder. Therefore he conducted experiments which led to the steel and wrought-iron cannons. His cannons were "built-up" in that the tube consisted of several parts. The tube was cast solid of heated and hammered steel. Once the bore had been drilled and the chamber completed, the tube was heated, then hardened and tempered by a plunge into rape oil. When the tube was cooled, coils of wrought iron were shrunk upon it, that is, wrought-iron hoops too small to fit over the tube's exterior circumference were enlarged by heating and placed over the tube. Upon cooling, the hoops shrank and compressed the tube. Part of the stress caused by firing, therefore, was transmitted to the hoops which preserved the tube. Although the system was sound, it was not until 1880, when various ways of working steel were perfected, that gunmakers could apply it with great success.

FIGURE 30. *U.S. 6-lb. field gun, bronze, Model 1840. (In general use throughout the Civil War.)*

When the Civil War began the Northern troops had few cannons, for the Confederates had seized a great part of the stores. The loss was not severe, because the government had never possessed many guns and the few it had were obsolete. As the Union cast about for weapons, it bought many of Sir William Armstrong's products, both of the breech-loading and muzzle-loading varieties. The most widely used field guns were the bronze 12-pounder pieces known as "Napoleon."

Sir Armstrong's method of locking the breech by

means of screwing the breechblock into the chamber, as opposed to Cavalli's wedge breech mechanism, was particularly successful. The screw was interrupted and the block's surface consisted of three or four sections of thread. Only half a turn was required to lock the breech. This method was adopted by the United States, England, and France, and it has been retained with some improvements. In the modern 16-inch coast guns the block's circumference is divided into sixteen parts, so that a greater portion of the block is locked by a slight rotation. To prevent any escape of gases through the breech, a pad is used which presses against the breech when the powder explodes and seals the space. Although the pad is of asbestos soaked in tallow, it dries up after continuous fire from fieldpieces. This system may leave something to be desired, but it is particularly satisfactory in guns of heavy caliber since it allows the use of separate ammunition (a type in which the projectile, powder charge, and primer are introduced into the chamber separately).

The Germans have retained the Cavalli wedge-breech mechanism. At first it was impossible to obtain any degree of obturation: some gases always escaped and caused the wedge to break. The metallic cartridge case furnished an excellent gastight seal by gripping the walls of the chamber when the powder exploded, and the Germans adopted it for cannon ammunition. The United States as well as Great Britain and France use this type of ammunition, called "fixed" and consisting of a metallic case which holds primer, powder, and projectile, only for 3-inch or smaller caliber guns. Ammunition for large guns is not of the fixed type, because the shell would be heavy and difficult to handle.

The reader will realize that in any kind of artillery, but specially in field artillery, one of the most important problems is to deal with the force of recoil. With the early cannon it was the practice to allow the trail to stop the recoil by its friction on the ground. Another way of checking recoil was to use the force to roll the carriage upon an inclined plane. The idea is still in use, although it has been translated into mechanical action. In some cases the gun was forced to raise a heavy weight placed and moving vertically to the carriage. During the middle of the nineteenth century the hydropneumatic recoil mechanism was perfected. This consisted of a cylinder filled with oil which was forced to pass through an opening in the pistonhead when the gun recoiled. To prevent the gun from returning to its firing position too violently, a spring served as counterrecoil buffer. A favorite type of recoil mechanism is the helical spring recuperator. From 1870 until the first World War we have used this spring recuperator in many of our guns. Although the Germans use it in their light as well as heavy and coast artillery and the British also favor the system for their heavy cannons, we abandoned it, because of our close association with the French Army during the first World War. We used the pneumatic recuperator sufficiently in the types adopted from French artillery to employ it in heavy coastal guns.

The pneumatic recuperator is really a modification of the hydropneumatic recoil mechanism mentioned above. It was developed by Colonel Deport, of the

French Army, between 1880 and 1890. It was first used in the famous French 75-mm. gun, Model 1897. The whole system consisted of the hydropneumatic recoil mechanism, that is, a cylinder filled with oil enclosing a piston to check the force of recoil. Instead of using springs as counterrecoil buffers, there is another cylinder in which a piston separates the oil and the air. The air chamber is

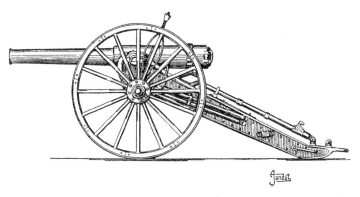

FIGURE 31. *U.S. 3.2-inch field gun, Model 1885–1897.*

liquid-sealed so that no air can escape. If there is any loss, it is one of oil, which can easily be replaced. The pneumatic recuperator furnishes an unusually long and moderate recoil and it lends stability to the carriage. Thus it has been found ideal for both field and heavy artillery. In spite of its conceded superiority, the French alone used the recuperator prior to our entry in the first World War. The Germans were unable to make it, and the English, even though they had the full co-operation of French engineers during the conflict, never adopted

the mechanism. Recuperators are such delicate instruments, requiring undreamed-of precision, that doubts
were generally cast upon our ability to duplicate them
in this country with our methods of quantity production
as opposed to the work of individually skilled French
gunmakers. Although we had trouble in translating the
French plans from the metric system to the system which
American industry uses, we gained enough experience

FIGURE 32. *U.S. 3-inch field gun, Model 1902.*

before the armistice to raise the art of gunmaking in the
United States to a perfection attained by no other country except France.

From 1885 to 1892 the United States Army developed
a 3.2-inch gun with a removable breechblock. Its recoil
mechanism was of the hydropneumatic type, with springs
to bring back the piece into battery or firing position. It
formed the bulk of the light artillery which we used in
the Spanish-American War. The advent of smokeless
powder necessitated the development of a new type:

smokeless powder burned over a period of time; the expanding gases did not furnish their maximum propelling power at the beginning of the explosion; the pressure of gases was equalized over the entire length of the bore and the bursting of cannons disappeared; the slow start of the explosion allowed the elongated projectile to grip the grooves firmly, and the turn of rifling was then made sharper to quicken the rate of the projectile's rotation. Thus smokeless powder made possible ranges that ridiculed all previous accomplishments, and it brought to the lightest gun a power which the heaviest pieces had never attained.

The United States Army adopted a 3-inch gun, Model 1902, for light field artillery work. It was first provided with the usual single trail, but in 1913, after much experimentation, the Ordnance Department suggested that the carriage be arranged with a split trail. The split trail allows greater elevation of the cannon, greater traverse (lateral movement of tube), and, by permitting more freedom in the movement of the tube, permits the gunner to sight a shifting target without continually changing the position of the carriage. The tube is of nickel steel and the breechblock, which is of the interrupted-screw type, is hinged to the rear of the tube. When the breechblock is opened, the firing pin, which it holds, moves to the side and returns to the firing position in the center of the breechblock upon closing. The recoil mechanism is of the hydrospring type. A cylinder, filled with oil and moving back with the tube when the gun recoils, encloses a piston held stationary to the cradle. The counterrecoil force is spent against springs. The gunners are protected by a shield. The piece fires fixed ammunition of two kinds, the steel shell and the common shrapnel.

As the chief weapon for our medium artillery, the United States Army adopted the 4.7-inch gun, Model 1906. It was completely of American design. The tube is built-up, and the breechblock is of the interrupted-screw type, with an extractor to throw out the shell case after firing. The firing mechanism, situated in the breechblock, is cocked and the firing pin released by pressing down the firing handle on the left side of the breech. The carriage has a single trail. The recoil system is of the hydrospring type, and it consists of a cylinder filled with oil to check the backward force of recoil and of springs to return the piece into battery. An armor-plate shield protects the gunners. The cannon has a maximum range of about 12,000 yards, and it hurls a 60-pound shrapnel as well as a 45-pound, high-explosive shell in fixed ammunition. During the first World War this field gun became motorized: the wheels were fitted with rubber tires and a 5-ton tractor tugged the weapon. We only had some sixty 4.7-inch cannons upon our entry into the conflict, but we ordered additional units, some of which were sent to Europe. The gun did not meet with much success upon the battlefield, where it was outranged by all the weapons of its class. Recently the Army has refitted the 4.7-inch gun, mounted it on pneumatic tires, and provided it with a split trail which allows much greater elevation and greater range. As a result of these improvements, this double-purpose piece has acquired unusual proficiency both as a gun and a howitzer.

When we declared war upon Germany in 1917 the Ordnance Department found it extremely difficult to procure field artillery pieces in quality and quantity sufficient for the needs of our vast new Army. We knew nothing of the 37-mm. cannon used by European foot soldiers to wipe out machine-gun nests. The gun is so small (its bore has a diameter of 1½ inches) that it can be handled by two men. It has a split trail which, along with a short front leg, forms a tripod from which the gun can be fired. The piece can also operate upon wheels. The barrel is of steel and the breechblock is of the Nordenfeld type, that is, it is seated within the breech where it rotates, thus opening and closing the chamber. The recoil mechanism is of the hydrospring type, one cylinder filled with oil and housing a piston to absorb the recoil and springs to soften the counterrecoil. It is equipped with a telescopic sight for direct fire and with a quadrant for indirect fire, thus making the gun highly accurate. Having a maximum range of 4,000 yards, it can fire fixed ammunition (high-explosive shell enclosed in a brass case, the whole weighing 1.47 pounds) at the rate of thirty-five per minute.

The gun was first developed by Major Garnier of the French artillery, and we became acquainted with it and adopted it as a result of our close association with the French Army during the first World War. We still use the 37-mm. in the Services where it is particularly useful as an antitank weapon. Our modern 37-mm. antitank gun, recently adopted, can fire ten armor-piercing projectiles capable of penetrating 1½ inches of the best armor plate at 1,000 yards per minute. One thousand yards is the most effective range against tanks which are not readily seen at greater distance. There are thirty 37-mm. guns (not counting those mounted upon our light tanks) in our modern armored division, eighty-four in the square division, sixty in the triangular division, and thirty in the Corps Artillery Brigade. At the end of the

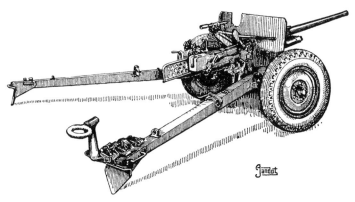

FIGURE 33. *U.S. gun, 37mm., M3 carriage M4. (Antitank gun.)*

first World War we had over two thousand such guns, and with recent production we face no shortage.

In 1917 we had five hundred and fifty-four 3-inch field-pieces, Model 1902. We were not tooled up to go into production. Since we were to co-operate with the French Army and since France was in a position to bolster the strength of our light field artillery, we decided to adopt the French 75-mm. (2.95-inch), Model 1897, which the Allies had used so successfully upon the European battlegrounds. The cannon is of the built-up type; its tube is of steel. The breechblock, like that of the 37-mm., is of the Nordenfeld type. The carriage is provided with the Puteaux or pneumatic recuperator. The recoil mechanism consists of two cylinders, one filled with oil and fitted with a piston, the other also fitted with a piston which separates the nitrogen and oil contents. The two cylinders are connected so that the flow or throttling of

FIGURE 34. *U.S. 75-mm. field gun, Model 1897 (French).*

oil from one to the other spends the force of recoil and softens the counterrecoil. The gun, which has a single trail, is seated upon steel-tired, wooden wheels, and an armor-plate shield protects the gunner. The 75-mm. fires fixed ammunition, the shrapnel projectile weighing 16 pounds and the high-explosive shell weighing 13 pounds.

In our eagerness to put every available weapon upon the battlefield in 1917, and because it was necessary that we should only have one type of light artillery firing the French 75-mm. shell, we modified our 3-inch type, Model 1902. We reduced the caliber to 75 millimeters and named it the 75-mm. gun, Model 1916. Although this split-trailed weapon compared favorably with any other unit of the same class, we discontinued its manufacture after World War I because we were literally swamped with deliveries of the French model. During the war some American factories were turning a 3.3-inch field gun for the British. We placed orders for the gun, revising the tube to take our 75-mm. ammunition. In 1935 we modernized it, equipping it with rubber tires and a tubular trail 8 inches in diameter. This weapon, known as the 75-mm. gun, Model 1917, is now used by our troops in Hawaii and the Philippines.

The greater part of our light field artillery now consists of the 75-mm. gun, Model 1897, which has been greatly modernized. It is provided with a split trail and a new carriage with pneumatic tires, which increase the elevation of the tube from 19 to 45 degrees, thus raising the range from 9,700 to 13,500 yards. The traverse or lateral movement has jumped from 6 to 85 degrees. In 1934 the Martin-Parry or Buquor adaptor became standard equipment. It is an instrument attached to the axle of the carriage to permit the replacement of wooden wheels by smaller pneumatic tires without altering the carriage or decreasing the elevation of the gun. The adaptor can be used for ammunition wagons as well as for the field gun, which can be towed over a road at 50 miles an hour. The 75-mm. gun now designated as Model 1897A4 is particularly useful as an antitank weapon; there are eight in each armored and triangular division and sixteen in each square division.

Most artillerymen insist that it is a wise step to match each field gun with a howitzer (a short cannon that de-

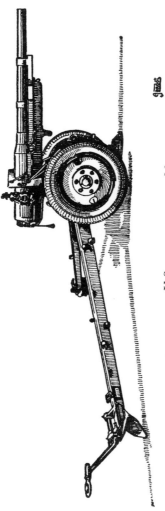

FIGURE 35. *U.S. gun, 75-mm., M2.*

livers high-angle fire with a curved trajectory) of similar caliber. To achieve this ideal, the Army has recently adopted a 75-mm. field howitzer, Model A1, provided with a split trail and pneumatic tires. A half-track truck tows the 75-mm. howitzer, and it can negotiate the roughest terrain to keep up and support the advancing troops. We have also recently adopted a pack howitzer for use in mountainous country. It is divided into parts, each one of which a mule carries. It fires a semifixed ammunition, that is, ammunition in which the projectile, the silken bags of powder, and the metallic case are brought up separately and assembled before firing. The weapon corresponds to the 2.95-inch (75-mm.) Vickers-Maxim mountain gun, which consists of a cradle, a trail, a gun, and the axle and wheels, each load being carried by a pack animal. It has a one-piece steel barrel, an interrupted-screw breech mechanism, and a hydrospring, recoil mechanism. So much for light field artillery and pack artillery.

In addition to the 4.7-inch, double-purpose gun, our medium artillery consists of two other weapons. The Army has adopted both only recently. The first is the 105-mm. field gun, M3; the second is the 105-mm. field howitzer, M2. Both are provided with high-speed carriages, including pneumatic tires, a hydropneumatic recoil system, and split trails. They fire fixed ammunition and are towed by a truck at a speed exceeding 50 miles. Since the two pieces constitute new ordnance, they would prove more than a match for German artillery of the same class.

When we entered the first World War we had little heavy artillery. In an effort to bring all our guns into

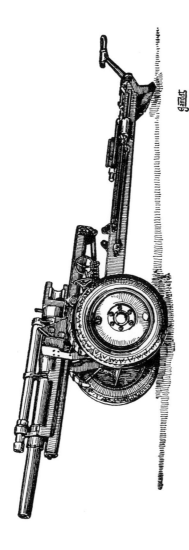

FIGURE 36. *U.S. howitzer, 105mm., M2 on high-speed carriage.*

action, we collected some twenty-eight 5-inch and one hundred and seventy-one 6-inch coast artillery and naval guns. We had to improvise wheeled mounts to carry the heavy weapons. The naval guns were shortened to an average length of 30 calibers (the length equals thirty times the gun's caliber), while the coast artillery pieces were left as they were with a view to returning them for coast service after the conflict. The 5-inch and 6-inch guns had a range of 9 and 10 miles respectively. We also used a 7-inch, .45-caliber naval gun mounted on a tractor and having a maximum range of 25,000 yards. Although these heavy rifles are not obsolete, they would not be used unless in a period of emergency.

In spite of the improvisations just mentioned, we did not have any heavy artillery worthy of the name. Our manufacturing facilities were not tooled up to produce large guns. Therefore, we adopted the French 155-mm. howitzer and gun. The 155-mm. howitzer, Model 1918, was originally manufactured by Schneider at Le Creusot. It could throw a 95-pound, high-explosive shell 12,530 yards, that is, over 7 miles; it hurled the shrapnel projectiles 10,835 yards away. One of the best howitzers used upon the European battle front, it was of the built-up type, having an interrupted-screw breech mechanism. At the breechblock a flexible asbestos ring served as obturator pad, for the pressure of expanding gases compressed it so that it sealed the breech to prevent gas leakage. This method was necessary because, separate ammunition being employed, there was no metallic shell case to secure obturation. The firing mechanism consisted of a primer fired by a firing pin which was driven forward by the hammer when the operator pulled the lanyard. The recoil mechanism was of the hydropneumatic type and consisted of two cylinders filled with liquid (glycerin, water, and caustic soda), two air cylinders, and a counterrecoil cylinder. The carriage was provided with a single trail. The 155-mm. gun (Grande Puissance Filloux), Model 1918, provided with a split trail, a similar recoil mechanism, and breechblock, had a muzzle velocity of 2,411

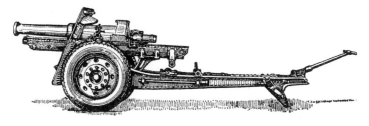

FIGURE 37. *U.S. howitzer 155mm., Model 1918 A1.*

feet per second and a maximum range of 17,700 yards. Both fieldpieces fulfilled their mission well during World War I.

We still employ the 155-mm. howitzer, Model 1918, but we have modernized its carriage by mounting it on pneumatic tires. It is towed at high speed by a 4-ton truck. We have completely changed the 155-mm. gun. It is mounted upon four sets of double-pneumatic and truck-size tires so that its prime mover can tow it at high speed. The new gun weighs 15 tons, has a muzzle velocity of 2,800 feet per second, and it can hurl a 95-pound projectile to a distance of 26,000 yards at a maximum elevation of 45 degrees. The backbone of our heavy field artillery, this weapon is the equal, if not the superior, of any gun in the same class used by any foreign power.

During the first World War we also acquired some 8-inch howitzers of British design. Now designated as Model 1918M3, they can hurl a 200-pound projectile some 11,750 yards. A 9.2-inch howitzer, also a British

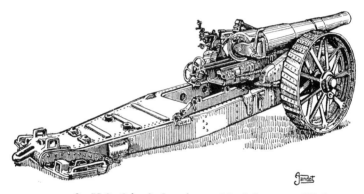

FIGURE 38. *U.S. 8-inch howitzer, Model 1917. (Vickers Mark VI.)*

model which we adopted during World War I, had a range of 13,000 yards. Although we still employ these heavy howitzers, our Army relies mainly upon the 240-mm. howitzer, Model 1918M1A1, which we acquired while fighting with the French. It was originally manufactured as a 280-mm. howitzer by Schneider, the well-known French gunmaker. The howitzer consists of four main parts: the barrel, the carriage, the cradle and the recoil mechanism, and the firing platform. Each part is carried by a prime mover. The howitzer is built up of alloy steel. The breech mechanism is of the interrupted-screw type fitted with an obturator pad. Like the 155-mm. class, the 240-mm. uses separate ammunition. Since the projectile alone weighs 356 pounds, it is loaded by means of a hand crane. The recoil mechanism, similar to that of the 155-mm. howitzer carriage, is of the hydropneumatic type. The piece has a range of 17,000 yards. Although the second World War has seen bigger weapons, it has seen few that were as powerful as the 240-mm. howitzer.

To complete the description of field artillery, mention must be made of the 6-inch trench mortar adopted from a British model. The weapon is similar in principle and constitution to the 3-inch Stokes mortar described in the previous chapter, except for two slight differences: one is in size, the 6-inch mortar being naturally much larger; the other difference lies in that the 6-inch weapon employs no bipod for support. It fires a projectile—a fragmented cast-iron shell with vanes weighing about 50 pounds—to a maximum range of 1,800 yards. This weapon is useful because of its curved trajectory, but it is seldom employed except in trench warfare.

CHAPTER SEVEN

RAILWAY AND COAST ARTILLERY

WHEN WE see a picture of a modern 16-inch gun that stands guard off our coasts, when we see the diminutive figure of a man tending the steel-spitting monster, we feel a certain amount of pride because the huge gun is a product of our industrial maturity. Yet there have been heavy guns before the industrial age, perhaps even heavier guns, although not as powerful. When the Europeans discovered the use to which they could put powder, they had comparatively little need of small weapons. Civilization was at a stalemate. Men and women lived and fought in medieval castles behind walls sometimes 6 yards thick. Wars were of the defensive type, consisting of laying siege to fortresses and walled citadels, of repulsing assaults and maintaining the fort. The attacker's main problem was either to scale or breech the wall, and he needed heavy guns to accomplish his purposes just as the defender required fortification pieces. Big guns, therefore, guns which could obtain the most destructive results out of powder, were in demand as early as the fourteenth century.

Large-caliber pieces were usually made upon the Continent, where gunmaking was more advanced than in England. The Dulle Griete, which the people of Ghent employed in 1411, was built around 1380. It had a length of over 16 feet and a weight of 13 tons. The diameter of the bore, that is, the caliber, was 25 inches, and the powder chamber had a bore of 10 inches tapering down to 6 inches. It fired a 700-pound stone ball. The range was naturally very limited, for the charge was roughly mixed black powder, a quick explosive which could not be used in too great quantities if the gun was to stand the shock. Curiously enough, the Dulle Griete's barrel was of the built-up type, consisting of an interior tube made up of lengthy wrought-iron bars welded together like the wooden staves of a wine barrel and reinforced by successive and continuous wrought-iron rings heated and shrunk upon the tube to compress it. Gunmakers followed this system probably because they could not cast iron for such huge pieces and because cast-iron tubes would have burst upon the explosion of a heavy black-powder charge. It is doubtful, however, whether the gunsmiths were aware of the scientific reasons for the advantages which the built-up system afforded.

The famous wrought-iron gun, the "Mons Meg," now found at Edinburgh Castle goes back to the middle of the fifteenth century. It had a caliber of 20 inches and hurled a stone ball of 300 pounds. The large guns were called "great bombards." Their range was limited to a few hundred yards. When besieging a castle, men would bring the piece towed by horses and would set it upon a cradle or wooden platform, point it toward the target, and fire its heavy stone projectiles until they breeched the wall.

Large guns also sat upon fortifications, at a port's

entrance or at a river's mouth, to deny passage to enemy
ships. They were set in fixed positions and their tremendous weight prevented both elevation and lateral
movements, so that the soldiers could not train them
against any special target. The gunners generally waited
until the enemy ship sailed before their line of sights to
fire their piece. The Turks used these guns as coast defenses to forbid the straits of the Dardanelles to foreign
sailing ships. When Sir John Duckworth sailed up the
narrow passage with a British naval squadron in 1807, the
giant bombards belched stone missiles that damaged six
men-of-war and killed over one hundred men. They were
cast of bronze at Constantinople as far back as the fifteenth century, and the Sultan of Turkey presented one
of them to Queen Victoria in 1876. It was 17 feet long,
weighed almost 19 tons, and consisted of two equally
large sections which were unscrewed to facilitate transportation. The bore had a diameter of 25 inches, wide
enough to house a granite ball weighing over 650 pounds.
What the projectile lacked in momentum was made up
by weight.

An even larger gun, known as the "Mortar of Moscow," was cast of bronze in the sixteenth century. It had
a length of 18 feet and a bore diameter of 36 inches tapering down to 18 inches at the breech. Its stone projectile
must have weighed a ton. Such a missile must have done
much damage, but it is surprising that gunners did not
cast metal projectiles before, since the small but dense
iron ball could do just as much damage as the unwieldy
stone. A small, forged wrought-iron or cast-bronze gun
throwing metal was as powerful as the cumbrous bom-

bard, and its mobility, the ease with which one could transport it and train it against a shifting target, was certain to cause the doom of the bombard as soon as metallurgy would be sufficiently advanced to lower the cost of metallic bullets.

The change occurred during the sixteenth century, when the art of working metals progressed far. The price of iron and bronze dropped, and armies could now afford to hurl heavy bullets at one another. The small guns with a caliber rarely over 5 inches appeared in increasing numbers to replace the bombards. Their power put an end to defensive warfare and the medieval fortress became obsolete; nobles learned to build their castles for architectural beauty, no longer for security. During the next century the thick walls surrounding stubborn lords' castles became playthings before the countless muzzles of the king's artillery. Guns were mounted upon wheeled carriages to follow the infantry. Large pieces gave way to the smaller types, even for fortification and coast defense.

Corn powder supplanted serpentine powder in the seventeenth century and cannons had to put on some weight to meet the stronger shock of explosion. While the small field guns were cast of bronze, the slightly heavier pieces were of iron cast around a core. Gunmakers began to mount their coast and fortification weapons upon wooden carriages rolling on four wheels. From the barrel's sides, trunnions protruded which held the gun to the carriage and which allowed some elevation when the gunner removed a wedge from under the breech. Most cannons were muzzle-loaders, although some breech-loading pieces were used on ships.

During the eighteenth century heavier guns were cast for coast defense. Most of them were muzzle-loaders and smoothbores, while there were a few rifled cannons and breechloaders. No special recoil mechanism existed; ropes usually held the weapons in place. Considerable improvement was made in carriages. Because of the increased accuracy of small arms, gunners had to operate from protected positions. A gun was usually fired through the embrasure of a wall. Late in the century carriages were such that one end pivoted in a fixed position under the embrasure, while the other end or the trail was mounted on a small wheel. This gave some traverse to the gun. A screw situated under the breech replaced the wedge system of securing elevation. In spite of the improvements contributed by five centuries, the coast gun of the eighteen hundreds was weak and inefficient compared to the weapon that more recent changes have made.

During the War of 1812 the United States used 8-inch and 10-inch cannons called columbiads, bulky pieces introduced by Colonel George Bomford. They were smoothbores of cast iron which could hurl solid shots and shells to protect distant positions. Heavier types were not used because they broke easily. As a matter of fact, cast iron was looked upon with suspicion. To remedy the defects of larger pieces, General Rodman of the United States Ordnance Department devised, in 1860, a new method of casting hollow tubes, a method according to which the interior of the tube was cooled first to secure hardness and uniformity of grain, while the exterior was kept at a high temperature. General Rodman succeeded moderately and furnished a 15-inch columbiad used in the American Civil War.

Another type known as the Dahlgren gun was employed during the Civil War. It was the invention of Lieutenant Dahlgren (1809–1870) of the United States Navy. Like its predecessors, the Dahlgren was a smoothbore of cast iron. Its distinctive feature was that the thick-

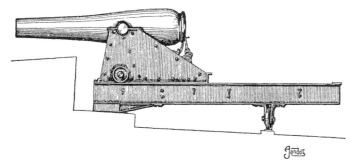

FIGURE 39. *Coast Artillery. 10-inch Rodman gun. Mounted on Barbette carriage. Circa 1863–1880.*

ness of the tube varied proportionately to the pressure of the exploding gases, the pressure being determined by experimentation.

Around 1845 the Cavalli and Wahrendorff systems of closing the breech by means of a wedgelike breechblock sealed the fate of smoothbores. It had been long recognized that a bullet spinning upon its own axis maintained its course for a greater distance and that the best means to impart the spin was to cut grooves in the bore. Rifling was only advantageous, however, if the bullet fitted so snugly in the bore that it prevented gas leakage and that its sides would grip the grooves firmly to receive the spin. To ram a bullet sufficiently tight down a muzzle-loader was too difficult, and a system of breech-loading had to be devised before gunmakers would look upon rifling with favor. Cavalli's and Wahrendorff's wedge system of breechblock allowed much gas leakage and had to wait for the development of the metallic shell case, which is the most satisfactory breech sealer because the case presses firmly against the tube's walls during the explosion. The metallic shell case for heavy cannons appeared after 1850. Germany, whose great metallurgists and gunmakers are the Krupps, is the only country to use the wedge type of breechblock and the metallic shell case (the ammunition must in this case be semifixed, that is, the case holds the base charge) to secure obturation. Other nations, such as the United States, Great Britain, and France, prefer to use the interrupted-screw type of breechblock with separate ammunition (no metallic shell case) for their high-caliber guns because fixed ammunition for large pieces is unusually heavy and difficult to handle.

Inasmuch as the wedge type of breechblock did not prove satisfactory until the metallic shell case came into use, another system was soon devised. It was the interrupted-screw type of breechblock invented by Sir William Armstrong. Although an obturator pad is now used to prevent gas leakage, it is not quite as satisfactory as the metallic case, at least from that point of view. In addition to his breechblock, Armstrong also produced a method of manufacturing built-up barrels. His method was an admission that in homogeneous guns, after a certain thickness has been reached, no additional amount of iron will increase the resistance of a tube. Armstrong took a tube and shrank hoops upon it, thus compressing the tube which would then transmit some of the explosion's stress to the surrounding hoops. Failures of guns were materially reduced, and this advanced method of

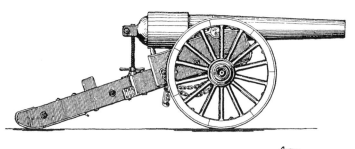

FIGURE 40. *U.S. 100-lb. Parrott rifled gun on siege carriage. Circa 1862–1870.*

building barrels along with the breech-loading system induced all nations to adopt rifling.

During the Civil War we employed some of Armstrong's breech-loading rifled cannons. In an effort to obtain the needed artillery we even bought some muzzleloaders, which Armstrong continued to manufacture because Great Britain had no faith in the breechblock systems. To simplify muzzle-loading, the English Government asked Mr. Whitworth to conduct experiments with oval and hexagonal twisted bores. Although there was no need to ram the bullet so that its sides would grip the grooves firmly, the new bores were not practical, for they emitted a missile, the irregular shape of which met too much air resistance to maintain a steady flight. With breech-loading and rifling firmly established, it was not long before the elongated projectile proved its advantages. The art of working steel and of making steel alloys became so advanced toward the end of the nineteenth century and the discovery of smokeless powder so reduced the shock of explosion that undreamed-of ranges were attained without barrel failures.

In 1885 the United States did not have the industrial facilities to forge guns over 6-inch caliber and so our large cannons were imported from abroad. At that time our warships carried 9-inch smoothbore and 8-inch rifled muzzle-loading guns. Some of the heavy Parrott pieces which we had used during the Civil War were converted for naval use. Our steel industry has since grown to unexpected proportions, and we have plants capable of turning out 16-inch rifles, or even larger if necessary.

Gun carriages improved considerably during the nineteenth century. We have seen how pivoting carriages were employed as early as 1800. The double carriage soon appeared, consisting of a regular carriage mounted on a lower carriage which had four wheels running on two circular tracks in front of an embrasure in the wall. When the lower carriage rolled completely to one side, the gun came within the fortification parallel to the wall, where the gunners could load it through the muzzle with safety. The accuracy of small arms became such that it was necessary to adopt a disappearing carriage, one which would permit the gun to drop behind a parapet so that

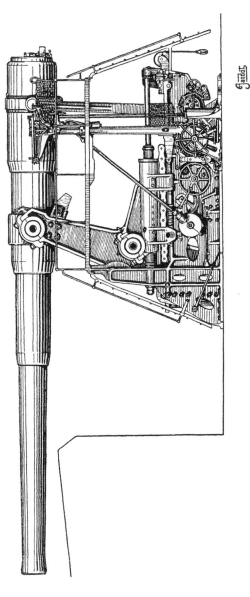

FIGURE 41. *Coast Artillery. 12-inch, Model 1895, rifle on Model 1901, disappearing carriage. (Type is still used in most coastal fortifications.)*

its gunners could load their cannons from a protected position. One famous system, known as the American Buffington-Crozier disappearing carriage, used in our fortifications from 1885 till the present day, consisted of a double carriage set in a cylindrical well. The lower carriage rolled on circular tracks and provided all-round traverse. When a shot was fired, the force of recoil raised a weight in the well and a latch locked the top carriage while it was at its lowest position, where it could be loaded in all safety. A hydraulic brake similar to the recuperator of field artillery was adopted to check the force of recoil.

More modern is the barbette carriage, which has been used for our large 16-inch, .50-caliber coast-defense guns. The guns are mounted in a cylinder or cradle which rests upon the side frames of the main carriage by means of trunnions. The main carriage revolves about a central pivot supported by rollers which travel upon a circular base. Thus, when the carriage turns, the gun turns with it and is endowed with all-round motion. A hydropneumatic recoil mechanism checks the backward movement of the gun and a pneumatic recuperator (sometimes springs) returns it to the firing position. Mortars are mounted in pits upon carriages similar to the barbette type.

Railway carriages originated in the American Civil War. General Robert E. Lee asked that some heavy guns be mounted on railway cars, protected by armor plate; the result was a 32-pounder. In 1864 the Northern forces besieging Petersburg fired a 13-inch, cast-iron mortar from a railway flatcar. Railway carriages made little headway until the first World War, when all the nations involved tried to bring as many heavy guns as possible to hamper the enemy's maneuvers. Officers had advocated that the United States adopt a system of railway artillery for coast defense, the argument being that the mobility of such batteries would multiply the effect which they

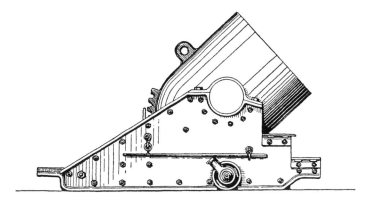

FIGURE 42. *U.S. 13-inch siege mortar. Circa 1840–1870.*

generally had at fixed emplacements. Upon our entry in the war we improvised various types of railway carriages to accommodate the artillery which we hoped to obtain.

The first type of railway carriage was called the "sliding" carriage. It was especially suited for heavy guns, which were mounted directly on the girders of the railway carriage by means of their trunnions. The guns were fired directly from the tracks, the recoil being absorbed by the sliding of steel beams against the railway ties.

Guns were also mounted on "rolling" carriages in which the recoil action was absorbed by the carriage's rolling back on its wheels until the brakes stopped the movement. With these two types, the guns had to be pushed back into firing position by soldiers. The guns could only

FIGURE 43. *Eight-inch gun on railroad mount, Model 1918.*

travel vertically since they only had elevation aim. To obtain lateral movement, the guns had to be rolled on curved railway tracks until the desired traverse aim was obtained.

The other two types, the emplacement and outrigger carriages, are still in use today and play an important part in our coast defenses. In the first, the gun is in its cradle, which is held to the side girders of the car by its trunnions. A pit is dug and filled with beams to form a firing platform upon which the mount is placed. It is similar to the barbette carriage and it allows all-round fire. The second type requires no foundation: the recoil is absorbed by means of spades driven into the ground. What most hampers our large-scale adoption of railway artillery for coast defense is that tunnels are in many instances too low to allow the passage of large rifles and bridges have not been built to withstand the weight of heavy artillery. The full use of railway artillery would necessitate a new coastwise system of railways, a very expensive proposition.

Although we have been experimenting with 18-inch rifles, our largest gun is the 16-inch, .50-caliber piece, Model 1919, mounted on a barbette carriage. The barrel is wire wound and has a length of about 70 feet. The projectile weighs 2,340 pounds and travels a distance of 31 miles when the gun is elevated to a maximum of 65 degrees. We also have a similar gun mounted on a disappearing carriage. Our 16-inch, .25-caliber howitzer, Model 1920, mounted on a barbette carriage, can hurl huge projectiles well over 15 miles. We have 14-inch, .40-caliber guns, some mounted on railway carriages, others upon concrete emplacements protected by armor-plated turrets. Able to throw a 1,200-pound projectile over 18 miles, they perform an important part in coast defense.

We have limited ourselves here to a description of the larger types. The United States Army has, of course, many other models, varying in caliber from 12 to 3 inches, some mounted on railway, some on barbette, and others on disappearing carriages. We certainly have no shortage of heavy artillery; what we have suffices amply for coastal defense.

The reader will perhaps remember that the Germans used a long-range gun to shell Paris during the first

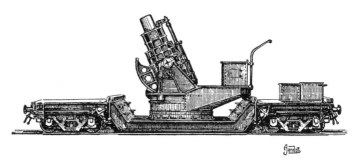

FIGURE 44. *U.S. 12-inch mortar, Model 1890, mounted on railway car, Model 1918.*

World War, a gun which could reach a target 90 miles distant. He may now wonder why we have no such weapons. The answer is that it is not practical. A heavy gun, like any other weapon, must be well balanced. The Germans employed a 210-mm. (about 8 inches) gun with the tremendous length of 140 calibers. This weapon had a muzzle velocity of 5,200 feet per second (usual muzzle velocity is 3,600 feet per second) and it hurled a projectile weighing only 264 pounds. The Germans rifled their projectile before inserting it into the bore, but the life of the gun was limited to fifty rounds. Al-

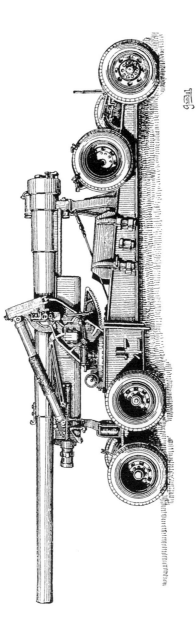

FIGURE 45. 155-mm. gun, M1, on carriage M1 (1941).

though the experiment was scientifically useful, the German long-range guns have little more than propaganda effects. The insignificance of the projectile, the difficulty of scoring hits, and the short life of the gun make the weapon of little value. The United States could also build such long-range pieces, but it has chosen a wiser policy in looking for the combination which will do the most damage.

CHAPTER EIGHT

ANTIAIRCRAFT ARTILLERY

AIRPLANES FIRST came into use as weapons during the first World War and, to follow the old, often-quoted maxim, it was necessary that some means of defense should arise to meet the new threat. Such was the origin of the new but highly complicated antiaircraft artillery. Prior to our entry in the war we had thought of antiaircraft guns only as supplements to our coast artillery. It had seemed obvious that we would first meet attacks from enemy airplanes upon our seashores. In keeping with this idea, the Ordnance Department had developed a 3-inch antiaircraft gun, a high-powered piece with a muzzle velocity of 2,600 feet per second. The only fault with the gun was that it fired from a fixed emplacement, and, since no airplane or zeppelin ever passed our coastline, we never had a chance to use it. The weapon was later placed upon a self-propelled mount of the seacoast barbette type, which allowed all-round firing and 90-degree elevation.

After the United States declared war upon Germany the Army immediately recognized the importance of mobile antiaircraft artillery as the best means of protecting the ground forces which we intended to send to Europe. We had done no work at all, and the situation was so pressing that the Ordnance Department did not have sufficient time to develop and test an entirely new type. We decided to improvise some antiaircraft artillery by mounting 75-mm. field guns, Model 1916, on 2½-ton White trucks. The mount became known as Model 1917. The gun had an elevation ranging from 31 to 82 degrees,

FIGURE 46. *U.S. 75-mm. field gun, Model 1916, on antiaircraft truck mount, Model 1917, 2½-ton White truck.*

and its traverse aim was 240 degrees, that is, the gun could revolve up to two thirds of a circle upon its own axis. It hurled a 15-pound projectile to an altitude of 6,000 meters. Naturally fixed ammunition was used, not only because it is our custom to use it in small-caliber field artillery, but also because separate ammunition would so limit the rate of fire as to check definitely the efficiency of the gun.

Antiaircraft artillery has always used fixed ammunition and it employs it more than ever today. The time fuse consisted of a compressed black-powder train ignited by the shock of firing and of such a length that the train would burn and ignite the detonator before reaching the plane. If the shell burst 50 yards away from the plane, some fragments traveling at high speed probably damaged the machine, although not fatally. The powder-train fuse was not as accurate as our modern mechanical time fuse, for powder burns at a rate varying with the altitude. The necessary compensating measures naturally involved errors and failures. The time fuse met with more favor than the percussion fuse, which would only cause the shell to explode upon hitting the airplane or upon falling back on the ground. Some percussion fuses were used in antiaircraft shells for the defense of London during the earlier part of the present war, and the returning shells caused almost as much harm to civilians as did the bomb splinters from the enemy planes which it was their mission to drive off. Another factor militating against percussion fuses for antiaircraft work is that only a direct hit will damage the flying ship, when a shell with a time fuse may burst sufficiently near to harm the craft, even though modern planes are heavily armored.

Inasmuch as the Ordnance Department had adopted the 75-mm. gun only as a temporary measure, we developed a high-powered, 3-inch antiaircraft gun, Model 1918, and mounted it on an auto-trailer carriage. Unlike the two previous types, the gun was not placed on a self-propelled mount. The weapon had a muzzle velocity of 2,400 feet per second, a maximum angle of elevation of

85 degrees, and a maximum horizontal range of 12,140 yards. The barrel was built up of nickel-steel forgings; its recoil mechanism was of the hydrospring type. This weapon was the best available at the moment, although we did not manufacture it in time to conduct trials in actual warfare. The airplane itself was entirely new in warfare: no nation was prepared to meet the threat; no nation had developed guns specially fitted for the work; all the warring countries had to improvise guns which did not even approach the specifications. No one should wonder why antiaircraft artillery made such a bad showing during the first World War. The conflict ended before the new guns, specially designed for antiaircraft work, could be brought into action.

The 4.7-inch antiaircraft gun, Model 1918, was one of the new pieces which had been developed and which was ready for manufacture when the signing of the armistice interrupted its progress. It had a maximum horizontal range of 15,000 meters and a vertical range of 10,000 meters. Its high muzzle velocity and the weight of its projectile would certainly have contributed toward making it a good gun.

The efficiency of an antiaircraft battery is limited by other factors than the weapon's possibilities. Thus the sight which we originally employed during the first World War was not provided with a telescope until General Pershing recommended its adoption. The instruments for finding the altitude and other firing data were so crude that they materially reduced the effectiveness of antiaircraft batteries. It is even doubtful whether the primitive artillery was worth its cost. It has been estimated that during the first World War an average of twenty-eight hundred shells were fired for every plane brought down by antiaircraft projectiles. If we place the normal cost of a shell at fourteen dollars, we shall see that to bag one plane set us back $39,200.00. Naturally, the figures are only approximate, but they do show that only the richest countries could afford protection for their civilians and their soldiers.

When the leading military powers were once more enjoying a well-earned peace after 1919, they returned to economy. The building program and the development of antiaircraft guns and fire-control instruments were stopped in the United States as in other countries. The primitive weapons which we had obtained sufficed for some years to come. In 1925, after the airplane had already proved that it was here to stay, especially for war uses, the government manifested some interest in antiaircraft defenses, and the Ordnance Department embarked upon a program which was to make our artillery of this type more advanced and complete than that of any other nation. The foreign powers, however, have surpassed us in the quantity, if not in the quality, of antiaircraft matériel as a result of the rearmament program which preceded the present war.

Our antiaircraft defenses consist now of varied weapons. Of course, the soldier carries either his Springfield or his Garand rifle, and he can fire—especially with the latter, which has a faster rate of fire—against any plane that gets within his range. Even the relatively inaccurate Browning automatic rifle can be of some use in a difficult moment. Modern planes, however, with their

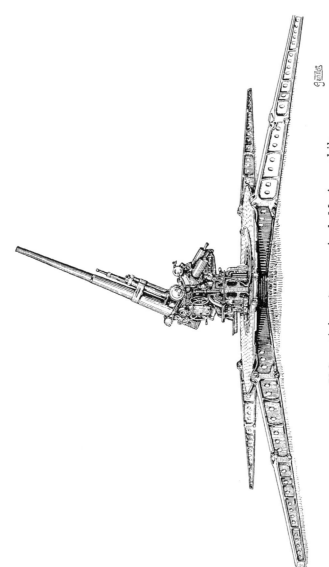

FIGURE 47. U.S. antiaircraft gun, 3-inch M2A2 mobile.

armor-plate protection and high-speed dive-bombing tactics present both an elusive and indifferent target. Antiaircraft machine guns of the Browning type have such a high rate of fire that they form a cloudlike dan-

FIGURE 48. *U.S. automatic antiaircraft gun, 37mm. M1A2 on carriage M3.*

ger area which airplanes hesitate to penetrate. The .50-caliber machine gun fires a sufficiently heavy projectile to keep airplanes at a respectful distance.

The need was always felt, nevertheless, for a weapon which would be light enough to accompany the troops and still fire a missile capable of damaging a plane. We have adopted, therefore, the 37-mm. antiaircraft gun. It is mounted on four pneumatic tires which spread and allow the carriage to lower and settle on the ground where outriggers hold it firmly. Two men aim the gun from steel seats, one sighting for elevation, the other for traverse. The weapon is fully automatic: it hurls a 1⅓-pound projectile at the rate of 120 per minute. The weapon is not on a self-propelled mount, but is towed by a truck. The fixed ammunition destroys itself if no hit is scored, so that it may not harm the soldiers upon returning to the ground. The 37-mm. antiaircraft gun is such a worthy weapon that factories are turning out many for issue to the troops at a rate of twenty-four units for each mobile antiaircraft regiment.

The British are now using a new, light antiaircraft weapon, the Bofors 40-mm. (1.57-inch) quick-firing gun. It is now manufactured for the United States Navy, and the Army has just adopted it to supplement the 37-mm. artillery piece. These light weapons protect the troops by discouraging low-flying planes. They are very accurate, but one hit as a rule will not suffice to bring down a modern bomber.

Until recently our large type of antiaircraft artillery consisted mainly of the 3-inch gun. This weapon is generally mounted on a firing platform of the barbette type, allowing all-round fire and 90-degree elevation. It fires at a rate of twenty-five shots per minute; each projectile weighs 12.7 pounds. Although its maximum vertical range is 9,700 yards, it is most effective at about 6,000 yards. It is evident that modern bombers can fly at higher altitudes, but the 3-inch gun keeps them at a distance from which accurate sighting and bombing are impossible. We have also been using a gun of larger caliber to reach higher altitudes, the 105-mm. antiaircraft gun, hurling a 33-pound shell at an effective vertical range of 9,100 yards, horizontal range being 21,000 yards. Our factories are still producing those two weapons to defend our cities and vital areas.

We have recently adopted two new guns, the 90-mm. and the 4.7 inch antiaircraft pieces. The 90-mm. (3.54-inch)—incidentally the French were using an antiaircraft gun of the same caliber—is intended for the mobile antiaircraft regiments, which will possess twelve guns each. The two weapons are now being turned out as fast as possible.

Of equal importance are the fire-control instruments, without which any antiaircraft gun is only a ghost. Probably the most important of these instruments, and undoubtedly one of the most complicated machines used in any line, is the director, a box provided with two telescopes to track enemy warplanes, to find their position, speed, and direction. The director computes all this information automatically once the correct altitude has been supplied to the machine. The altitude is determined by an equally intricate instrument, the optical height finder.

The task of antiaircraft batteries is increased many times at night, for it is more difficult to locate high-flying bombers hidden by clouds and nocturnal obscurity. To achieve this, gunners use a triple-eared sound locator which is mounted on a platform and can revolve up to

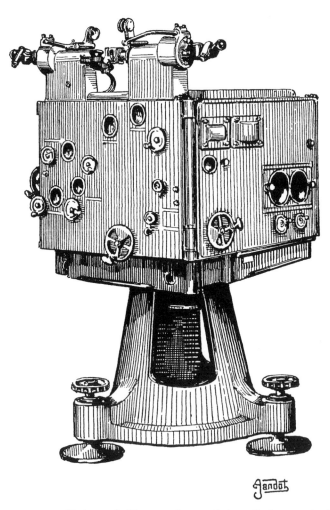

FIGURE 49. *Universal director for antiaircraft fire control.*

360 degrees. The giant and sensitive ears amplify the sound of droning motors and locate the enemy crafts. One cannot aim a gun by sound locator alone, for sound

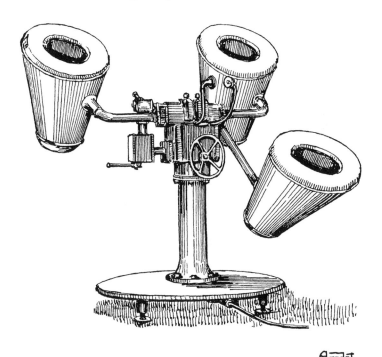

FIGURE 50. *Modern sound detector for antiaircraft fire control.*

waves travel too slowly and allow the airplanes to shift their positions. The sound locator is sufficiently accurate, however, to direct the 60-inch mobile searchlight once the huge candle's shutters are opened. It is relatively easy for the searchlight to spot the bomber against which the gunners proceed as though it were daylight. The fire-control instruments travel in trucks, and a

Jandot

FIGURE 51. *Modern antiaircraft searchlight. 60-inch Sperry reflector with an 800,000,000-beam candle power.*

power control truck, provided with generators and cables to feed electricity to the various machines, accompanies the battery.

The greatest shortcoming of fire-control instruments is that their cost is too high—prohibitive, except to the richest nations. The antiaircraft guns are also very costly.

The shells which our new guns hurl into the sky are provided with mechanical and watchlike fuses which raise the price of one projectile to fifteen dollars. Although antiaircraft protection is expensive, it is well worth while since it saves both human lives and property. The reader must not forget, however, that in the greatest aerial struggle the world has ever witnessed, in the battle of England, only part of the planes brought down have fallen victims to antiaircraft guns. Nor must the reader forget that it would take much antiaircraft artillery to defend effectively the New York metropolitan area and much more to protect all our cities. And effective defense by antiaircraft weapons merely implies keeping enemy planes at an altitude so high that they will not be able to pick out military targets. That is no mean accomplishment, of course.

CHAPTER NINE

TANKS AND OTHER MECHANIZED VEHICLES

WHAT COMES to the average person's mind whenever he reads or hears about a tank assault or the movement of a motorized unit? A vision of speed immediately appears before his eyes, of speed, our partial answer to the invulnerability of time and space. He realizes that warfare has kept up with our achievements, that its weapons have been endowed with the mobility of our means of transportation, that tactics have quickened, that a campaign can now cover in one month as much territory as Napoleon covered in a year. In the average person's mind the tank is engraved as a symbol of speed, and speed itself is the essence of modern warfare, perhaps of our civilization.

When one sees a car racing at 80 miles an hour, however, one must of necessity understand that speed is only one requisite, for there are few tanks which will reach 40 miles per hour, even on favorable terrain. Speed is not even the major consideration. It is subordinated to other factors essential if the purpose of the weapon is to be carried out. The mission of the tank—as it was during the first World War and is still today—is to transport a certain amount of fire power while affording maximum protection to its operators. Thus fire power and protection are two prerequisites to the fulfillment of the mission. To be sure, transportation is almost as important and transportation involves speed; but the relative value of speed decreases after a certain limit. The three elements, therefore, which all tanks possess in varying degree are protection in the form of armor plate and elusive shape, fire power obtained through armament like machine guns or cannons, and mobility, which includes maneuverability as well as speed. Some of these elements are contradictory. It is evident that, given limited horsepower, any increase in armor-plate protection will raise the weight of the tank and reduce its mobility. A compromise must naturally be arranged. As the relative importance of each element is emphasized, the nature of the mechanized vehicle can change from a tank to a combat car or a scout car.

The tank was a weapon born of the first World War. It was designed and built by the British Navy as a land ship called "tank" to baffle enemy agents. Although the first types differed widely in shape and construction, they all embodied the same principle—the use of the track. The track was invented by an American named Holt around 1900 and was first used on tractors as farm implements. The track is driven by a sprocket. The wheels of the tank actually roll upon the track and advance as the links in the track successively strike the ground. The tracks were delicate instruments, but they enabled a vehicle to negotiate rough terrain.

The British Army was the first organization to employ the tank as an engine of war when it led the attacks in the Somme sector in September, 1916. It was a daring innovation, and the British only made it in an attempt to break the stalemate reached in the war. The tremendous fire power of modern machine guns, rifles, mortars, grenades, and even field artillery had forced both the Allies and the Germans to dig trenches for protection. Every assault upon a trench, every attempt at taking a machine-gun nest resulted in such heavy losses in men that, even if achieved, the gain was not worth the cost. Armies, therefore, chose to lie under cover, to fight a war of attrition. The British perceived that if, in an assault, the men could bring sufficient fire power under protection to bear upon enemy emplacements, the war would become one of movement to be decided either one way or the other, but quickly. The tank, as developed by the British Navy, was the answer. The motor would take care of the transportation problem, the tracks would caterpillar their way over trenches and obstacles, and armor plate would afford the protection behind which the gunners would pour machine-gun fire upon the enemy. The first British experiments did not meet with much favor because the tanks employed were much too bulky. They weighed over 40 tons and moved at walking pace. Their motors often broke down, affording fine targets for the German field guns. As the war progressed, however, the tank evolved, and when the United States entered the conflict it was definitely an important tactical factor.

When we declared war upon Germany in 1917 we found that the Allies were using two different types of tanks. The British favored the heavy land ship capable of accommodating a crew of twelve men, while the

French adhered to the small, two-man model. We decided that much could be said for both systems and, as a result, adopted a light and a heavy tank. The French tank, of the Renault type, was sufficiently satisfactory to warrant our copying it immediately. The American copy, Model 1917, was a 6-ton weapon manned by a

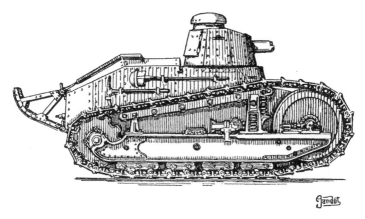

FIGURE 52. *Six-ton tank, Model 1917 (Renault type).*

driver and a gunner. Its power plant consisted of one Buda 4-cylinder motor. It had an approximate length of 16 feet, but its width was not quite 6 feet. Its maximum speed was 5 miles per hour and it could climb a 45-degree slope. The model was naturally protected by armor plate. Some of the tanks were mounted with a 37-mm. cannon, while others carried a Marlin tank machine gun, caliber .30. It was a slow but effective weapon, even though each one of the machines cost us about eleven thousand dollars.

As for the heavy tank, the British were so little pleased with their own weapon that they advised us to develop our own type. The British staff furnished general specifications which our product had to meet to be of fighting value. The result was a 35-ton tank with a 300 horsepower, 12-cylinder Liberty motor as a power plant. Its armament consisted of two 6-pounders mounted in

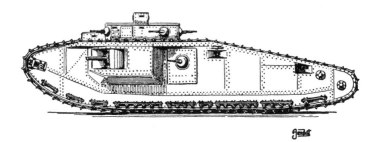

FIGURE 53. *U.S. tank, Mark VIII (35-ton, crew 11 men, armament two 6-lb. cannon and seven machine guns), 1918.*

sponsons (protrusion on a ship's side) on each side and of seven machine guns, caliber .30. The tank was over 34 feet in length. It had a maximum speed of 6 miles per hour and was capable of climbing a 45-degree slope. The land ship was separated by a wall situated in the middle, thus making a fighting compartment in the front and an engine room at the rear. A crew of eleven soldiers manned the tank, one of them being an officer who commanded his men and directed all operations from a conning tower or small turret which gave him all-round observation; he communicated with his men through tubes. One driver steered the tank as easily as though it had been a truck by means of two brakes, one for each track. To turn the machine, the driver merely slowed one track or stopped it entirely to do an about-face. All the orders placed for this tank were in the process of construction when the armistice was signed; none was tested in actual combat.

Two new types of tanks were adopted before the armistice, namely, the 3-ton machine and a 6-ton machine. The 3-ton tank was manufactured by the Ford Motor Company, which expected to turn out one hundred daily in 1919. It was almost 14 feet in length. Two Ford motors, geared together, each drove a track and achieved a maximum speed of 10 miles an hour and a climbing ability of 45 degrees. The crew consisted of a driver and a gunner; the latter operated either a Marlin tank or a 37-mm. cannon, according to the use for which the tank was destined. Its small height (5 feet 4 inches) and its mobility made the 3-ton tank an elusive target not easily discernible and of great value in rough terrain.

The 6-ton tank, which was to succeed the Renault machine, was a cheaper weapon, one more adaptable for large-scale production, yet superior in fighting power. Its crew of three men had command over a machine gun and a 37-mm. cannon. Considering the primitive development of the automotive industry, its speed of 10 miles an hour was remarkable. The power plant consisted of a 60-horsepower, 6-cylinder Hudson motor. Neither the 3-ton nor the 6-ton tank ever reached the European battle front, but it is evident that they were by far superior to the weapons of any warring country.

As soon as the first World War ended the nations of

the world forgot about the new weapon. Peace was the hope of everyone. All engines of war were looked upon with disdain. It was only after a few years that experiments were resumed. Progress in the automobile indus-

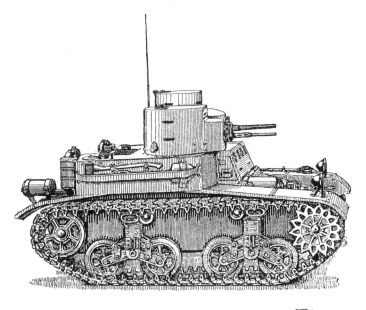

FIGURE 54. *Light tank, M2A2 (1934). Armament, one .50-cal. machine gun, two .30-cal. machine guns.*

try and the mechanical as well as technical soundness of the caterpillar armored vehicle forced governments to develop the weapon. Moreover, there was a definite trend in the early twenties against large armies, and the only alternative, as advocated by such men as General

De Gaulle, was the organization of a small but motorized force.

The United States has always favored, at least in normal times, a small peacetime army, augmented by the National Guard and Organized Reserves. Partly because of the lack of funds, partly because some elements in the Army were attached to horses, hardly more than thirty tanks were built in the United States during the decade and a half that succeeded the armistice. These tanks differed widely; they were experimental models, pilot types to guide future production should war ever come again. The first was adopted in 1922. It was a medium tank which weighed approximately 23 tons and which had a length of 21 feet 6 inches. The period following was one of extreme economy as far as military affairs were concerned, and it was not until 1928 that the next model appeared. It was a light tank, weighing 7½ tons with a length of about 13 feet. Its revolving turret, unlike other models, was perched at the rear of the machine, while the power plant worked at the front. This system was followed in the construction of the 15-ton medium tank, Model 1929, but it was abandoned in the 11-ton medium tank, Model 1930.

As the automotive industry progressed, the Ordnance Department devised new types. For instance, a combat car weighing 8 tons came out in 1932. During the following year two medium tanks, one of 15 tons and the other of 13 tons, were tested. In 1935 the Army adopted two light tanks, one weighing approximately 9 tons while the other was as light as 3 tons. The latter distinguished itself because of its low silhouette and maneuverability. Until that time our Army had not adopted tanks in any quantity, but the rearming of European nations, and more particularly the present European conflict, has forced the United states to embark upon a huge tank-building program. Since we never had ordered any tanks from private manufacturers, at least since the first World War, no factories were tooled up to go into quantity production, and of course this factor has slowed down our program considerably.

We are now using seven different types of light tanks, ranging from 16,675 to 22,900 pounds in weight. Their average speed is about 30 miles an hour whereas the average speed of French light tanks in 1939 was about 12 miles an hour. Their length varies between 13 and 15 feet. Some of our light tanks have one turret which carries a 37-mm. cannon and two .30-caliber machine guns. Other machines are mounted with two turrets carrying one .50-caliber and two .30-caliber machine guns. The machine guns are naturally air-cooled and recoil-operated Browning weapons. The crew consists of three men, one driver and two gunners. The average light tank can climb a 20-degree slope if the ground is muddy and a 25-degree slope if the ground is dry. All types, however, can climb a 45-degree slope whenever the crew attaches the grousers to the tracks. The average tank maintains a speed of 15 miles an hour while negotiating a 5-degree climb. To reduce the effects of friction, the tracks and the track idlers (the little wheels which roll upon the tracks) are rubber-coated.

Manufacture of some of the types mentioned above has been stopped in favor of a new light tank, M2A3 or M3, Model 1938. It is armed with either a 37-mm. cannon or a .50-caliber machine gun accompanied by .30-caliber machine guns. It has a speed of 35 miles an hour, a speed much higher than that of any light tank pos-

FIGURE 55. *U.S. medium tank, M3, 28 ton (1941). Armament consists of six guns, the largest of which is a 75-mm. cannon.*

sessed by any country. Although it is dangerous to mention figures which change from day to day, we have on hand a considerable number of tanks of all types and the monthly production is rapidly growing. We also have some combat cars (M1), which resemble light tanks and which carry one .50-caliber machine gun, two .30-caliber machine guns, and one Thompson sub-machine gun. Many of these vehicles carry a rope or towline ready for use in case of a breakdown.

Medium tanks are generally heavier and therefore slower machines. Although we have built experimental models, we never ordered medium tanks in any quantity before the present emergency. Now, however, we have several sources of supply, among the largest being the A. C. & F. plant at Berwick, Pa., and the Chrysler Corporation at Detroit. The tank which we used in 1940 weighed 21 tons. In spite of its heavy armor-plate protection, it was capable of traveling at a speed of 32 miles an hour. A high-velocity, 37-mm. cannon mounted on a revolving turret and eight machine guns make up the armament. It was the equal, if not the superior, of the tanks which were used in the European conflict, but we are no longer manufacturing it.

To replace the 21-ton medium tank, the Army has recently adopted a new machine, the 28-ton, medium tank M3. This is a speedy weapon, speedier than the machines of the same class now being used by Germany, Russia, and Great Britain, speedier perhaps than those nations' light tanks. It carries a crew of seven men and, like our new light tank, is fitted with a radio which facilitates communication between fighting units and which may prove a decisive factor in tactics. For its size, our medium tank is also believed to be superior in armament to what Germany has. It is mounted with a 75-mm. gun which has been shortened, with a 37-mm., high-velocity cannon, and with a few .50- and .30-caliber machine guns.

The reader may have deduced from preceding paragraphs that we have no heavy tanks. Indeed we have not, at least not yet, according to our designations. The Army considers any vehicle up to and including 15 tons in weight a light machine, while tanks up to 30 tons are called medium tanks. We should remember, however, that designations are relative. Five years ago—and according to European standards—any vehicle up to 10 tons in weight was light, up to 20 tons medium, and anything above 20 tons heavy. Nevertheless, no matter what designations we use, we have nothing to match the 80-ton machines which France once had or the huge monsters which Germany and Russia display in parades in Berlin and Moscow respectively. As a matter of fact, Russia may have some 100-ton land ships armed with cannons heavier than our 75-mm. gun. The Germans are said even to have some heavy French tanks captured in 1940, to have removed their superstructures and to have fitted them with 105-mm. guns. The question is: how maneuverable are the giants? How far will they go without bogging down? It is obvious that when they break down they make a target which gunners would have difficulty in missing. The answer is not to emphasize either armament or size, but to secure a proper balance between protection, mobility, and armament, while keeping an eye upon the tank's mission.

The tank may be the backbone of the armored forces, but there are many other mechanized vehicles which play an important part. First is the gun carrier, a small machine stressing speed and fire power at the expense of protection. Until recently we had only a few gun carriers. To remedy the defect the government has recently obtained a few Bren gun carriers from Canada. It is a caterpillar machine, fully tracked, mounting a .50-caliber automatic gun of special design. The British have used the Bren gun carrier in their African campaigns

FIGURE 56. *Half-track personnel carrier T1E1 (1933).*

with great success, and the Army is putting it through trials to see whether we should adopt it or a machine of similar design.

In 1937 the Army adopted a scout car mounted upon heavy rubber tires and protected with armor plate. It is armed with one .50-caliber machine gun and one .30-caliber machine gun, both of which can travel on a rail running around the car. We also have a half-track personnel carrier which can negotiate any terrain and lend infantry support to advancing tanks. It is armed with one .50-caliber and two .30-caliber machine guns to protect the car from attacking airplanes. Of course, there are also numerous motorcycles, sidecars, transport trucks, reconnaissance and staff cars.

Although at present the numerical strength of our

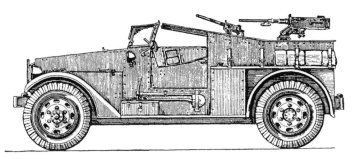

FIGURE 57. *Scout car, M3 (1937), mounting both .30- and .50-cal. machine guns on track mounts.*

mechanized forces is far from being satisfactory, it is rapidly growing. More and more tanks roll out of the factories, and we will soon have armored and motorized divisions second to those of no other country. One of the most promising factors is the wealth of experience which we have had with machines and motors since the last war. Another encouraging item is that we have profited from the lessons of 1940 and of 1941. The Germans have not performed their blitzkrieg before sightless men. We are now mastering the methods of fighting with motorized units. The matériel which goes to our troops is new in design. It has been evolved as a result of the campaigns in Europe as well as in Africa, and our equipment embodies the best qualities and not the faults of the tools that the warring nations have used.

CHAPTER TEN

ARTILLERY AMMUNITION AND AIRCRAFT BOMBS

THE FIRST missiles to come out of guns were balls of stone. They were light when compared with metal projectiles and did not create as much damage, but their cheapness maintained their popularity as late as the sixteenth century. Stones as heavy as 600 and possibly 2,000 pounds were hurled against fortifications by the huge bombards. Smiths knew how to cast metals into balls, or for that matter into any object, and the probability is that some solid shot of wrought iron and later of cast iron were used as early as the fourteenth century. The supply of refined metals, however, was too limited to warrant their use while stones were to be had for the asking. As soon as smiths learned how to work iron ore, furnaces sprang up and cast-iron balls came into favor. Cast-iron balls had just appeared when someone thought of firing the balls red-hot to spread conflagration wherever the so-called "hot shot" landed. The Confederate Army shelled Fort Sumter with hot shot during the Civil War.

Before cast-iron balls appeared, gunners sometimes employed earthen shells, hollow spheres of earth or clay hardened by heat, filled with black powder or with pitch and naphtha to frighten the infantry or spread fire over their equipment. Wrought iron forged into semispheres, which were filled with black powder and screwed together, served as shells. When smiths learned how to cast iron into hollow balls, the shell became an important projectile and remained in use as late as 1870. Even the 15-inch columbiad made under the supervision of

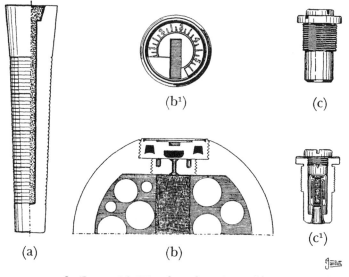

FIGURE 58. *Fuses. (a) Wooden time fuse. Circa 1700–1850; (b) (b¹) Bormann on 12-lb. shrapnel. Circa 1850–1870; (c) (c¹) Hotchkiss percussion fuse. Circa 1878.*

General Rodman around 1860 hurled spherical shells filled with black powder, the whole weighing over 250 pounds. All these spherical shells, whether they were earthen, forged, or cast, carried a crude fuse which the flash from the cannon's discharge ignited so that it might start the explosion of the shell's contents.

A Dutchman named DeWitt devised in 1666 a special shot for use in naval warfare called the "chain shot."
Two metal cups connected by a long chain fitted within
were hurled against the sails and masts of the wooden
crafts. As early as the fifteenth century, gunners began to
fire canister shot, consisting of a tin can or metal called
canister and containing a number of musket balls. The
whole was fitted to a wooden sabot or base, and it broke
upon leaving the muzzle, thus scattering death in the
ranks of charging infantry. Grapeshot appeared almost
as early. A number of balls or grapes, arranged in super-
imposed rows and separated by retaining bands, the
whole mounted on a metal base, broke loose upon leaving the muzzle. The balls varied according to the bore's
diameter and came in sizes large enough to bring much
destruction. Grapeshot was used widely until the nineteenth century, so widely that when the French adopted
the machine gun they called it the *mitrailleuse* (*mitraille,* grapeshot) because it sent hails of bullets much
like a grapeshot-throwing cannon (see Chapter Four).

It happened quite often that gunners did not even
bother to use previously prepared ammunition. They
inserted black powder in their muzzle-loaders, poured
quantities of loose musket balls or any missiles that
came within reach, rammed the whole charge tightly,
and waited for the enemy's assault. Canister and grapeshot, however, served their purposes only at short ranges;
only the cast-iron shell could reach the foe over long
ranges. To remedy the situation, Lieutenant Shrapnel
of the British Army invented in 1793 the projectile
which has taken his name. The original shrapnel shell

was a hollow cast-iron ball with an opening through
which a light charge of black powder and lead balls was
poured. It was only intended that the charge should break
the sphere into fragments sent whirring at a sufficient
velocity to incapacitate personnel. The gunner generally
cut the fuse so that it would only burn during the pro-

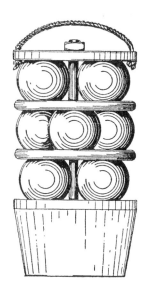
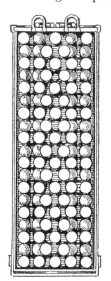

FIGURE 59. *Left, grapeshot circa 1840–1870. Right, case shot
or canister circa 1800–1880.*

jectile's flight. Although we no longer employ the spherical shrapnel shell, we have adopted its system for the
elongated projectile.

As long as the cannons were smoothbores, the pro-

jectiles had to retain their spherical aspect for the simple
reason that the weight of a ball is evenly distributed,
that air resistance affects all portions equally, whereas
an elongated, cylindrical missile tumbles over unless
maintained in its course by rotating upon its own axis.
Spherical shots were employed in rifled bores as well,

(b)

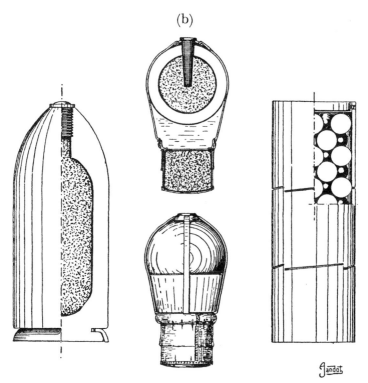

FIGURE 60. (a) Parrott 100-lb. shell, circa 1860–1870; (b)
Fixed spherical case shot with wooden time fuse; Sawyer
canister 3.2-inch cal., circa 1885–1900.

although by the nineteenth century gunners generally recognized that a cylindrical shot would spin better. The real difficulty lay in finding a scheme by means of which the elongated projectile could become practical, for most cannons were muzzle-loaders into which it was almost impossible to ram a missile sufficiently tight to allow it to grip the grooves firmly. Naturally there existed some breechloaders prior to the Cavalli and Wahrendorff system, but they did not close sufficiently tight to prevent the escape of gases. Moreover, when a projectile fills the bore snugly, so that it may fill the rifled grooves which are to impart the spin, it prevents the escape of the gases, and, until it is forced out, creates a pressure which can break the barrel of cast-iron guns. Thus gunmakers had to continue to manufacture muzzle-loaders as late as the middle of the nineteenth century.

To ease the muzzle-loading operation, the elongated projectile was often coated with lead. This scheme was not satisfactory, however, because lead was too soft to impart spin to the missile, which tore through the barrel without following the grooves. The lead also filled the grooves, and it was difficult to keep the bore clean. Another method was then tried. The base of an elongated projectile, smaller than the bore, had a leaden base which the gas pressure flattened and forced into the grooves. In 1865, Hotchkiss came out with a system which was altogether too complicated for manufacture. The base, propelled by the explosion, acted as a wedge and pushed the leaden rings of the projectile into the grooves. Shells were also cast with recesses to house lugs. The lugs were arranged in rings, as many in each ring as there were grooves in the bore. The recesses so weakened the shells, however, that the system was abandoned.

The British tried an ingenious idea in the Crimean War. Instead of using grooves to spin a projectile, grooves difficult to clean and constantly wearing away, they attempted to spin the projectile by means of a twisted oval bore, a bore of which any section was oval. The projectile was naturally oval and twisted to fit into the bore through the muzzle. Another system originated by Mr. Whitworth involved a hexagonal bore.

As soon as Sir William Armstrong perfected the building of steel and wrought-iron cannons, as soon as the breechblocks were sufficiently advanced to permit breechloading, the elongated, cylindrical projectile was widely adopted. The cylinder was of cast iron or of steel with a band of soft metal, usually copper, around the base to fit into the grooves. Projectiles have changed little since that time. We use armor-piercing missiles, since ships, tanks, and even airplanes have donned steel for protection. The pointed section of the projectile is only a windshield, an empty cone of steel which covers the blunt nose of the real projectile. The pointed windshield meets only a minimum of air resistance. When it strikes armor plate, even at an angle, it is quickly crushed and allows the projectile to strike squarely without deviating, whereas a pointed missile of solid steel would ricochet upon hitting the plate. This method is specially used for high-caliber guns, particularly those of seacoast and naval organizations. For smaller guns the same effect is sometimes obtained by adding a faked point of lead to a blunt-nosed bullet.

Powders fall into two general classes: propellants and explosives. Propellants burn over a period of time and their effect is not sudden, but cumulative. Smokeless powder, which most nations use today, is the ideal propellant because it is a slow starter. Explosives burn quickly, violently; their effect is felt upon the moment, like a punch, and they are ideal for blasting, not as a driving force. Black powder is really an explosive, and the failures of many guns may be traced to its use as a propellant. The effects of a black powder explosion in a cannon's chamber were felt like a blow. The projectile was thrown out all of a sudden, while what was needed was a powder whose gases would start slowly, multiplying in volume, expanding, and exerting increasing pressure as long as the projectile remained in the bore.

There were some attempts at controlling black powder to achieve the desired results. In 1880, in the Lyman-Haskins cannon, a single tube was provided with several separate and minor powder chambers branching into it which were to discharge as the projectile cleared their mouth. In another effort to create the gases gradually, General Rodman, in 1860, recommended that powder be formed into cylinders having a diameter equal to that of the bore and drilled with lengthwise holes. The combustion was somewhat slowed, but it was still too violent. In 1880 naval officers devised "cocoa powder" by decreasing the percentages of sulphur in black powder and substituting a half-burned wood for charcoal, which gave it its brown color and hence its name. The wood was never completely oxidized by the explosion, and cocoa powder left too much smoke and ashes. The first satisfactory propellant was smokeless powder, which is still used today. Its history and characteristics have been fully treated in connection with rifles (Chapter Three).

The high explosives which we use in our shells are of four types: trinitrotoluene (T.N.T.), ammonium pic-

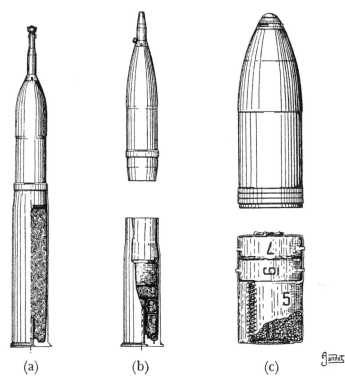

FIGURE 61. *Types of Artillery Ammunition.* (*a*) *fixed ammunition;* (*b*) *semifixed ammunition;* (*c*) *separate loading ammunition.*

rate, picric acid, and amatol. Trinitrotoluene, first made in 1880 by the chemist Hepp, results from nitrating toluene (obtained as a by-product of coke furnaces and artificial gas manufacture) with a mixture of nitric and sulphuric acids. Picric acid, a derivative of phenol, is practically insensitive to shock and is used in armor-piercing shells. It reacts readily with metals from which it is separated by shellac coats or by vulcanized fibers. Ammonium picrate results from the treatment of picric acid with ammonia. It is as insensitive as its mother acid and much more stable. Ideal for armor-piercing projectiles, since it will go through a 12-inch armor plate without exploding because of the shock, it is detonated by a booster—an intermediary agent between the fuse and the main charge—filled with tetryl (manufactured from benzene), after the shell has gone through the armor. Amatol is a mixture of ammonium nitrate and trinitrotoluene. We have other explosives, but they are of less importance.

Our ammunition falls into three classes: fixed ammunition, semifixed, and separate loading ammunition. In the fixed type the shell's base is inserted into a brass container or case which is fitted with a primer containing the propellant. In separate loading ammunition, the shell is inserted into the gun's chamber, followed by the propellant in silken bags and the primer. Fixed ammunition is used for guns up to 4.7-inch caliber. To break the load into parts for the sake of maneuverability, larger guns fire separate ammunition. There is also a semifixed ammunition, the metallic case being unattached to the projectile. The projectiles now used are of three kinds: the high explosive shell, the shrapnel shell, and the armor-piercing shell.

The fuse, whose function is to ignite the bursting

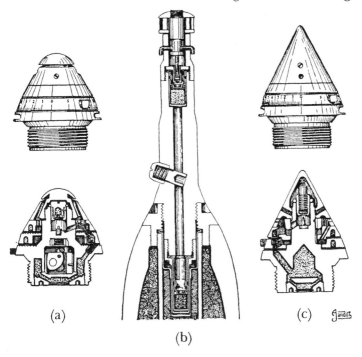

(a)

(b)

(c)

FIGURE 62. *Fuses.* (a) *Model 1907, 21 second combination time and percussion fuse (Scovill type)*; (b) *Mark III, point detonating superquick fuse with bore safety, booster, and detonator*; (c) *Mark II, type "S," mechanical antiaircraft time fuse.*

charge, is an important part of the projectile. A reed tube filled with serpentine powder was used in the first earthen shell. In the eighteenth century beechwood

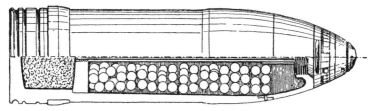

Model 1902, 3-inch shrapnel with 21 second time fuse.

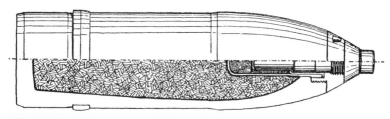

Model Mark I, 75-mm. high-explosive shell, with Mark IV percussion fuse.

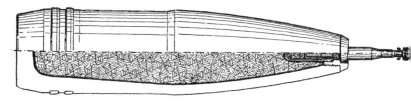

Model Mark III, 155-mm. high-explosive shell, with Mark III percussion fuse.

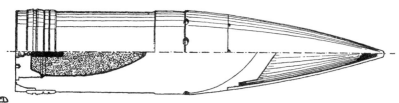

Model 1920, 16-inch armor-piercing shell, with base fuse.

FIGURE 63. *Shells.*

tubes filled with black powder were used as fuses. One could set the time for explosion by cutting the fuse to the required length. Metal tube fuses, filled with slow-burning powder and of varied lengths, were employed until well after our Civil War. There are now three kinds of fuses: time, percussion, and a combination of time and percussion. Some are attached to the projectile's base while others are at the point. Safety devices are provided for all fuses. Either the speedy flight or the rotation of the projectile is needed to free the firing pin so that it may come into contact with the primer. Thus the fuse cannot function until the shell has been fired. There is also a "bore safe" device, according to which the bursting charge is separated from the detonator until the shell has cleared the bore.

The manufacture of artillery ammunition is complicated and expensive. Constant experimentation is carried on, not only to improve explosives and the methods of handling them, but also to develop new designs in the shape of shells and the quality of the metals employed.

AIRCRAFT BOMBS

Bombers play such an important part in modern warfare that to supply them with ammunition has become a major function of the Ordnance Department. There are different types of bombs, varying with their mission. Explosive bombs are classified as demolition, fragmentation, and practice bombs. There are also chemical bombs, some to cause fire, others to lay smoke screens, and still others to incapacitate personnel in some manner. Of course, inert or drill bombs containing no explosives at all serve for training purposes. The practice bombs have a small quantity of explosives so that airmen can spot their hits. When practice bombs have no explosive charge their fins are painted in black to make them visible.

Bombs range in weight from 17 to 2,000 pounds. The lighter bombs are attached under or within the planes

FIGURE 64. *A 1918 model Glenn Martin bomber.*

either in a vertical or horizontal position. The heavier bombs travel in the horizontal position. All bombs are provided with a fuse, without which they cannot be detonated. They are shipped to the airdromes without the fuse, which is added as the ground crew loads the plane. All fuses carry a safety mechanism to prevent the functioning of their parts. When the bomb is placed under the aircraft an arming wire is attached to those parts. As the pilot releases the bomb he retains the wire, thus removing the safety device. The fuse mechanism starts to function immediately. The pilot can also release his load safely, especially if he is flying over friendly territory, by allowing the arming wire to follow the mis-

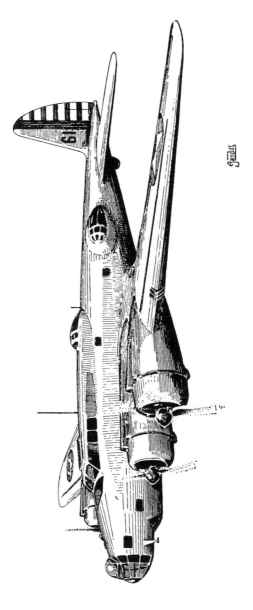

FIGURE 65. Flying fortress. Boeing bomber B-17.

sile. The standard arming wire is of hard-drawn brass, and its diameter varies with the weight of the bomb to which it is attached. This system was used during the first World War and is still the best safety device.

Demolition bombs destroy matériel by the sheer vio-

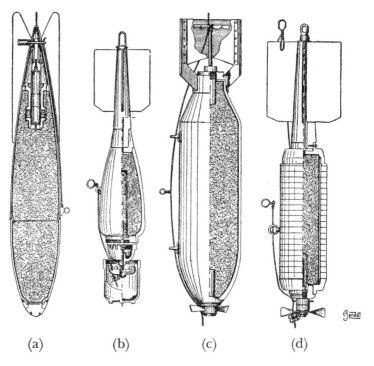

(a) (b) (c) (d)

FIGURE 66. *Aerial Bombs. (a) Mark III, 100-lb. high-capacity demolition bomb with percussion tail fuse (1918); (b) Mark III, 25-lb. Cooper fragmentation bomb with mechanical percussion nose fuse (1918); (c) M30, 100-lb demolition bomb with percussion nose and tail fuses; (d) M5, 30-lb. fragmentation bomb with percussion nose fuse.*

lence of their explosion. Their weight ranges from 100 to 2,000 pounds. They are all painted yellow to signify their purpose and are arranged in horizontal racks provided with two suspension lugs. The lightest demolition bomb, the 100-pound M30, used against railway matériel and ammunition dumps, is cylindrical in shape

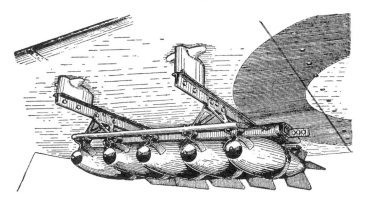

FIGURE 67. *Mark V, bomb release rack on a D.H.4 plane of 1918.*

with fins at the tail to maintain it in flight. It contains 57 pounds of high explosive, for the frame of a demolition bomb is as light as possible. It is the charge which performs the mission; the frame is subordinate. Another 100-pound bomb contains as much as 66 pounds of high explosive. The 2,000-pound drop bomb is designed for targets like battleships, dams, heavy bridges, and a conglomeration of buildings. It encloses 1,077 pounds of high explosive. Demolition bombs are the most widely used missiles, especially by bombers whose mission is to destroy military targets.

Fragmentation bombs are intended for use against concentrations of personnel or animals. Sometimes a group of airplanes waiting on the field will be torn to shreds by the numerous fragments traveling at high speed. These missiles are relatively light, no types weighing more than 30 pounds. The explosive charge is of minor importance, the ideal being to secure the most effective fragmentation. Unlike the demolition bombs, which are provided with both nose and tail fuses, the fragmentation bombs carry only a nose fuse. Since they are relatively light, these bombs require only one suspension lug to attach them to the plane.

Chemical bombs are of three kinds: gas, smoke, and incendiary. They are classified as having either a persistent or a nonpersistent filler. A nonpersistent filler is one which gives better results when it is not scattered over a wide area so that it will get the opportunity of mixing and reacting with the air. This type requires only a bursting charge capable of breaking the steel envelope. A persistent filler is one which performs best when diffused widely and which requires a heavy detonating charge. All chemical bombs carry out their mission better when they explode slightly above the ground; they are therefore provided with a nose fuse for quick action. Chemical bombs are painted gray. Inasmuch as they weigh only 30 pounds, they are attached by one suspension lug, either on a vertical or horizontal rack.

Practice bombs are as heavy as 100 pounds. They contain a spotting charge to facilitate the training of

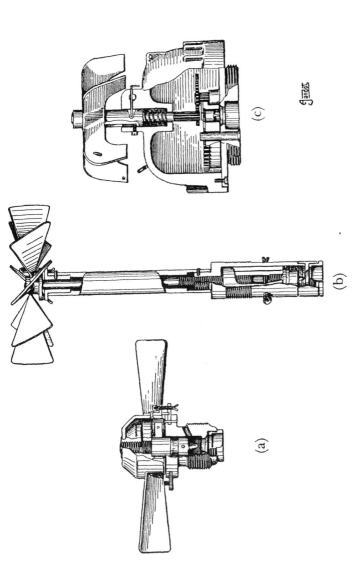

FIGURE 68. *Mechanical arming, Vane-type percussion bomb fuses. (a) Nose percussion fuse, Mark VII M1; (b) Tail percussion fuse, Mark V M1; (c) Cooper nose percussion fuse, Mark XII.*

pilots. The spotting charge only produces smoke. Practice bombs are usually painted blue and are sometimes loaded with uniform sand. Drill bombs also exist to train ground crews in handling the diverse types of aircraft missiles.

All the different types of bombs have one thing in common: they need fuses to cause their detonation. These are of two general classes, the nose fuse and the tail fuse. The first forms an integral unit with the primer, the detonator, and the booster. With the exceptions of time mechanisms, nose fuses function when the firing pin strikes the primer as the bomb hits the ground. Tail fuses are integral with the primer and the detonator. They function by inertia, that is, when the bomb strikes the target the firing pin continues to travel and hits the primer. Demolition bombs are provided with both nose and tail fuses, while fragmentation and chemical bombs carry only the nose type.

Fuses are also classified according to the method of arming: (1) the arming vane type; (2) the arming vane type with mechanical delay; (3) the arming pin type; (4) the arming pin type with time delay; (5) the time type. They can all be released safely so that the bomb may fall without functioning. The explosive element of most arming vane fuses is supplied by a shotgun blank cartridge. As soon as the bomb is released, the arming wire is removed, thus allowing the arming vane, which looks like an airplane propeller, to rotate by the force of air. The unscrewed vane falls off, disks are ejected, and the firing pin is in a position to strike the primer as soon as the bomb hits the target. In the arming-pin type the arming pin is ejected once the bomb is released. The detonator is pushed into firing position and is ignited upon impact. The other fuses differ in that they can be set either for instantaneous or delay action.

The reader probably realizes how intricate are the mechanisms which cause such destruction. New types are always being evolved. A new fuse or an unknown explosive is brought to bear and spread havoc. Thus the Royal Air Force has recently claimed successful performances with new superbombs. Airplanes have so increased their load capacity that they can carry tons of explosives in a single flight, and, since aircraft and flying as a whole is still a relatively new weapon, we are led to believe that what we have so far achieved is only a beginning. Whereas our artillery can reach targets 30 miles distant, airplanes, which serve the same purposes perhaps even more accurately, have an almost unlimited range. Our new artillery has wings.

CHAPTER ELEVEN

THE ORDNANCE
DEPARTMENT

THERE WAS a time in the history of military affairs when no agency, not even a single official, existed either to procure or distribute the tools of war. Certainly the man who broke off a branch from a tree, sharpened one end, and used it as a lance in times of conflict with either men or beasts did not need assistance in procuring weapons. Even the medieval knights ordered their bright armor, smooth shield, and sharp blade from a smith skilled in tempering metals, and, although they and their slaving peasants had to pay a burdensome fee for the manufacture, they came upon the battlefield armed from head to foot, ready to follow the king to whom they owed allegiance and fighting service. The knight naturally had to supervise and pay for the smith's work; yet he could readily persuade his peasants to contribute voluntarily a prescribed portion of the funds needed to equip a man-at-arms.

The longbow made the armored knight anachronistic; the crossbow, like our modern antitank gun, stemmed the onrush of charging steel; and the harquebus, with thunderous detonation of its powder charge, literally scared the horses out of their wits. The knights surely were not long to admit the uselessness of armored protection and to discard what they already looked upon as a heavy, cumbrous, suffocating metallic gear. However, when it came to recognizing that horses were more of a liability than an asset they were not so enthusiastic. Noblemen could not very well picture themselves hobbling about a battlefield like underfed peasants: not only would they tire more quickly, but their dignity would suffer just as much, if not more. It was not fitting, moreover, that they should stand behind a capricious gun piece, soiling their hands and fashionable battle dress with black-powder dust. Thus they clung to their horses and abandoned powder and its weapons to men with meaner claims to social distinction and with less regard for propriety.

As the harquebus replaced the sword, as the infantry asserted its superiority over the cavalry, as the weight of numbers played an increasingly important part in tactics, the little man, the common foot soldier, became all important. He was not rich enough, however, to buy his own weapons, and the party which employed him had to supply the guns and the powder. Thus every state was forced to form an organization or at least to delegate an agent to supervise both the manufacture and distribution of arms. As the weapons increased in importance and complexity, the ordnance agency had to evolve in size and technical ability to meet the requirements, and what was once a loose civilian organization has become a body of experts with well-defined duties.

At the beginning of the Revolutionary War certain committees of the Continental Congress performed the duties of the Ordnance Department. In 1775, upon appointing General Washington to the command of our colonial forces, the Continental Congress created the office of Commissary of Artillery Stores. Although General Washington was to choose him, the officer was a civilian. His job was more or less to store the supplies obtained by a committee of Congress. In 1776 a Board of War and Ordnance was set up to procure, care for, and distribute all the ordnance matériel needed by the armed forces.

The first man chosen from the Army to carry on the work was a colonel of Artillery appointed as Surveyor of Ordnance in 1789. Of course, Congress passed bills from time to time authorizing the President or his secretary of war to rent or even construct arsenals and to contract for matériel with private manufacturers. Congress created the Ordnance Department in 1812 to assist the Commissary General of Ordnance with his deputies and assistants numbering no more than thirteen. The Department had to procure, store, maintain, inspect, and distribute guns and ammunitions. Three years later, in 1815, soldiers skilled in mechanics were attached to fighting units along with carriages and the tools necessary to maintain and repair their equipment.

In 1821 the Army was reduced to a small peacetime force and the Artillery assimilated the Ordnance Department. The Department reappeared after eleven years and was placed under the command of a colonel with 13 officers and 250 enlisted men. It has functioned ever since that time, increasing the strength of its personnel and the expertness of its men to meet the requirements of modern arms and of crises like the Civil and the Spanish-American Wars. At the beginning of the first World War the Department consisted of 97 officers and 1,241 men. It was composed of four staff divisions (the Chief Clerk, the Administrative Division, the Accounting Division, and the Mail and Record Division) and three technical operating divisions (the Small-arms and Equipment Division, the Gun Division, and the Gun Carriage Division). Shortly after our entry into the war the Automotive Division, the Nitrate Division, and the Trench Warfare Division were added, and the Department increased its personnel strength to 4,527 officers and 25,054 men, along with a large number of civilians employed in arsenals.

In 1918 the Ordnance Department was reorganized along functional lines. The staff divisions gave way to the General Administration Bureau, the Engineering Bureau, and the Control Bureau, while the technical operating Divisions were replaced by the Procurement Division, the Production Division, the Inspection Division, and the Supply Division. This reorganization did not make for efficiency and the old setup was re-established with two main operating divisions for manufacture and supply.

The Ordnance Department of today functions very much along the same lines, although minor changes in its organization have been made to keep up with the increasing importance in warfare of the airplane, the tank, and the automatic gun. The mission of this service is to procure and distribute all the fighting equipment which the Army needs. Procurement includes design, development, purchase, manufacture, and test, while distribution implies storage, issue to the troops, maintenance, and repair. The fighting equipment becomes more varied and complex from year to year, and Ordnance matériel now embraces small hand and shoulder weapons, machine guns and automatic arms, field, coast defense, and antiaircraft guns and their carriages, ammunition, combat vehicles, and fire-control instruments.

To fulfill such exacting duties the Department has 350 officers and 4,500 enlisted men in time of peace. The present emergency and the exigencies of the program for national defense have made it necessary to increase sharply the personnel. Naturally a large number of civilians are employed not only in the manufacturing and repairing arsenals but also in the offices. Only a year or two ago practically no Ordnance matériel was manufactured by commercial industry, for the needs of our small peacetime force were amply satisfied by the supplies remaining from the last war. Much of the Department's work was experimental. For instance, the new Garand rifle was developed at the Springfield Armory over a period of fifteen years. The Department expected to meet the demands of an emergency by carefully preserving the matériel left from the last war, by continuing to manufacture arms in government arsenals, and by devising a procurement plan which would outline the means of placing commercial industry on a wartime footing.

The Ordnance Department was organized upon a basis fitting both war and peace so that the only change which the present emergency has made necessary has been one of expansion. The whole Department, officially known as the Office of the Chief of Ordnance, is under the authority of the Chief of Ordnance, who is a general officer. In order to carry out its mission of procurement and distri-

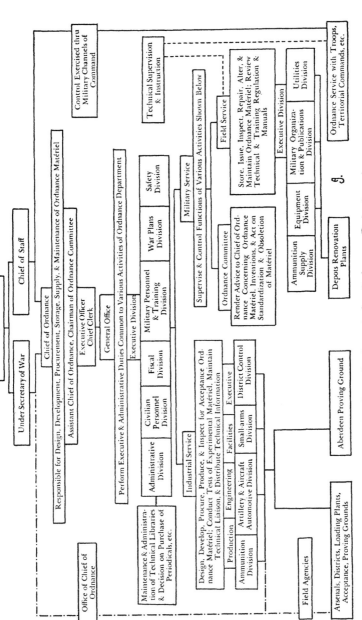

FIGURE 60. Organization of the Ordnance Department

bution, the Office of the Chief of Ordnance is divided into the three following groups: the General Office, the Industrial Service, and the Field Service.

The General Office performs the executive and administrative duties common to all the groups. An executive officer directs the work, as well as a public relations officer who maintains public and press relations, publishes official literature, releases matériel to foreign governments, and acts as liaison officer with other branches of the Army. The General Office consists of six divisions: the Executive Division, which co-ordinates the activities of the office of the Chief of Ordnance; the Administrative Division, which publishes all the departmental orders, bulletins, and circulars, arranges the printing of official publications, maintains office service, and distributes the correspondence; the Civilian Personnel Division, which arranges for the employment, service, pay, discharge, and working conditions of civilian employees; the Fiscal Division, which prepares estimates and presents them to the War Department Bureau of the Budget, apportions the departmental funds, supervises the business methods of the entire department, advises on legal matters, records all legal documents, and maintains liaison with the Chief of Finance and the Judge Advocate General; the Military Personnel and Training Division which directs the assignment, classification, and promotion of officers and enlisted men and supervises all the school training operations under the control of the Chief of Ordnance; the War Plans Division, which assembles the mobilization plans of the Department, determines the supplies required in case of mobilization, and issues lists of stocks on hand; the Safety Division, which makes recommendations for the safety of both personnel and property, keeps in touch with industrial safety practices, enforces safety rules by inspection, and approves the planning of new plants. Each of the six divisions has to furnish mobilization plans for their activities.

A former group was the Technical Staff. It rendered technical advice to the Chief of Ordnance, maintained technical liaison, disseminated technical information, and tested experimental weapons. It had to keep informed on the new matériel being used abroad and suggested at home, and whenever it found anything which might fill the Army's needs, it recommended it to the Chief of Ordnance. The Technical Staff fostered studies on new matériel, analyzed inventions, and conducted trials. It also prepared firing tables and ballistic data. To carry on its various functions, the Technical Staff was organized into four divisions: the Executive Division, which supervised and co-ordinated the activities of the other divisions, controlled the operations and the personnel of the Aberdeen Proving Ground, and administered the technical library of the Ordnance Department; the Ammunition Division, which carried on the duties of the Technical Staff with reference to bombs, grenades, pyrotechnics, and all ammunition above caliber .60; the Artillery, Aircraft and Automotive Division, dealing with cannons, carriages, carts, caissons, tanks, armored cars, tractors, and fire-control equipment; the Small-arms Division, which handled pistols, revolvers, rifles, machine guns, pyrotechnic projectors, and all ammunition up to and including caliber .60. There was also an Intelligence

Section which forwarded requests for information to the Military Intelligence Division of the War Department General Staff. The Technical Staff was rescinded in July, 1941, and all its duties were transferred to the Industrial Service.

The Aberdeen Proving Grounds, the largest land and water area allowed to the Industrial Service for proof testing of experimental matériel, is situated on the western shore of Chesapeake Bay about thirty miles from Baltimore. It has a land range of thirty thousand yards, and for testing heavy artillery that range may be extended another thirty thousand yards over water. It maintains a flying field for the purpose of testing bombs. It also has facilities for running tanks and gun carrriages over different kinds of terrain.

The second group is the Industrial Service, whose job is to design, develop, procure, and inspect all ordnance matériel. It must plan for procuring supplies in times of war by constructing new plants or expanding the facilities furnished by commercial industry. It must also test experimental matériel, maintain technical liaison, and disseminate information. The Chief of the Industrial Service has four assistant chiefs: one to supervise all production activities, the second to direct the Service's engineering activities, the third to control the construction of new plants and the expansion of existing facilities, and the fourth to direct the inspection activities of the Service. The Industrial Service is composed of five divisions: the Executive Division, the District Control Division, the Ammunition Division, the Artillery, Aircraft and Automotive Division, and the Small-arms Division (the three last being matériel operating divisions).

The Executive Division, in addition to co-ordinating the work performed by other sections of the Industrial Service, supervises the activities of the procurement districts and administers in a general fashion the manufacturing arsenals, the loading plants, and the acceptance proving grounds coming under the Service's control. The District Control Division supervises and co-ordinates the Service's procurement planning. It directs the procurement activities not only of the arsenals but also of the district offices. These offices number fourteen and are scattered throughout the country, in cities such as Boston, New York, San Francisco, so that the burden of procuring or manufacturing the enormous amount of supplies needed in wartime may be shared by all sections according to their capacities.

The main problem of the Industrial Service is to convert existing facilities producing peacetime articles into plants that will manufacture war products. It is the job of the district offices to survey the productive facilities of their section so that the assistant secretary of war may allocate them. When a survey of a specific plant has been made, the government makes an agreement with the plant officials, who signify their willingness to furnish upon contract in time of emergency certain items at a specific rate. If changes of the machinery or expansion of its plant are deemed necessary, detailed plans are made. Thus it has been possible in the present emergency for the government to sign a contract with the Eastman Kodak Company to manufacture shell fuses. These activities, which the district offices carry on and which the District Control Division supervises, come under the heading of "procurement planning."

The three matériel operating divisions (Ammunition, Small-arms, and Artillery, Aircraft and Automotive) of the Industrial Service conduct research in the design and preparation of new or experimental matériel. They store and maintain experimental matériel and inspect the procured matériel before it is issued to the Army. They also supervise the progress which commercial industry makes in the manufacture of orders placed by the assistant secretary of war.

These three divisions also supervise the work of the arsenals manufacturing matériel coming under their classification. The Watertown Arsenal, which is located near Boston, Massachusetts, manufactures the carriages for the heavy mobile field and railway guns, for the antiaircraft and coast defense guns. It has special manufacturing facilities for the production of hollow gun castings and maintains a large metallurgical laboratory. Watervliet Arsenal lies near the Hudson River, north of Albany. It was built in 1813 and until 1890 was an ammunition plant. Since then it has been the Army's cannon manufacturing center, from which come field, antiaircraft, and coastal guns (not including carriages) ranging from 37-mm. to 16-inch guns. Its activities after World War I were limited to making experimental and Navy guns, but in the present emergency it is working at full capacity. Rock Island Arsenal is situated on an island in the Mississippi River near Davenport, Iowa. It manufactures light and medium gun carriages, recoil mechanisms, and certain parts of the tank, scout, combat, and armored cars which it assembles. The

Springfield Armory, located at Springfield, Massachusetts, in operation since 1794, manufactures rifles (specially the Garand rifle), pistols, and automatic weapons. It conducts research work in small arms. The Frankford Arsenal, which is situated near Philadelphia, makes ammunition not only for small arms but also for artillery. It also manufactures fire-control instruments and gauges. Finally, there is the Picatinny Arsenal in New Jersey which produces fuses, pyrotechnic, smokeless powder, and other explosives in addition to conducting research.

The third group of the Ordnance Department is the Field Service, one of two main branches, the other being the Industrial Service. The general functions of the Field Service, which has the most personnel, are to store and issue ordnance matériel and to administer the field establishments which must inspect, repair, and maintain the supplies in storage and in the hands of troops. The Chief of Field Service is a brigadier general, and he has under him an Executive Division, an Ammunitions Supply Division, an Equipment Division, and a Military Organization and Publication Division. The Executive Division, in addition to co-ordinating and maintaining records of the Service, regulates the activities of the depots and repairing arsenals coming under the Field Service's control. It also deals with enlisted and civilian personnel. The Ammunition Supply Division controls storage, issue, and preservation of ammunition, and defines the regulations to be followed in handling it. It keeps records of stocks and applies for replacement or augmentation of matériel on hand.

The Equipment Division supervises the storage, issue,

and maintenance of all matériel except ammunition. It prepares lists of supplies needed for replacements and develops plans for the automatic supply of units in action. The chief duty of the Military Organization and Publication Division is to prepare war plans for the operation of ordnance units. It must also supervise, within the powers of the Chief of Ordnance, the activities of the ordnance units away from their training centers. In order to carry on its functions of storage and repair, the Field Service has control over depots and repairing arsenals scattered all over the country.

The Field Service also has remote technical control over the ordnance units which follow the troops, for these units are integral parts of the organization to which they are attached. They are men specially trained and equipped to repair and maintain in fighting condition the equipment of the troops. There are three different kinds of ordnance units: the medium maintenance companies, the ammunition companies, and the depot companies. The medium maintenance company is assigned to the infantry division. Because its mission is to repair the division's equipment and because it must operate at the front as an integral part of the division, the maintenance company has both a military and a technical organization. It is organized along military lines like the infantry company for questions of administration, discipline, and defense, and every man receives the same basic training as the infantrymen. Technically it is composed of men specially trained in the various skills necessary for repairing rifles as well as tanks. The medium maintenance company, which consists of one hundred and forty enlisted men, is led by a captain and five officers. For technical purposes it is divided into five sections: the Headquarters and Supply Section; the Service Section; Artillery and Automotive Section; the Armory Section; and the Instrument Section.

The Headquarters and Supply Section is headed by a second lieutenant and consist of eight noncommissioned officers and fourteen privates. It is equipped with a motorcycle and four trucks. A second lieutenant commands the Service Section which consists of a staff sergeant, a sergeant, and twenty privates and which is equipped with a pickup truck, a cargo truck, a machine shop truck, a tool and bench truck, and a welding truck. Its mission is to operate a machine shop to do the work that is beyond the scope of the other sections. The Artillery and Automotive Section consists of an artillery unit and of an automotive unit, each under the command of a first lieutenant. The artillery unit consists of a staff sergeant, a sergeant, a corporal, and twenty-four privates; it is equipped with a pickup truck, an artillery repair truck, an emergency repair truck, and a spare-parts truck. The automotive unit consists of a technical sergeant, a sergeant, a corporal, and twenty-seven privates; it is equipped with a pickup truck, an automotive truck, an emergency repair truck, a spare-parts truck, and a wrecking truck. The job of this section is to maintain the division's artillery pieces and vehicles. The Armory Section consists of a first lieutenant, a technical sergeant, a sergeant, a corporal, and sixteen privates; it is equipped with a pickup truck, an emergency repair truck, a small-arms repair truck, and a spare-parts truck. Its duty is to repair rifles, machine guns, and automatic weapons. The Instrument Section is under the command of a technical sergeant and is composed of a staff sergeant and eighteen privates. It has an instrument repair truck and must maintain fire-control equipment, sighting devices, watches, and tripods.

The medium maintenance company serves the division. Three medium maintenance companies form the ordnance battalion maintenance, which is assigned to the corps. Thus we see that the Ordnance Department not only procures the matériel needed by our fighting units, but it also follows those units, even in the combat zone. It operates machine shops at the line of battle and it maintains in fighting condition all the equipment that is needed in a campaign, from the smallest pistol to the heaviest tank. The Ordnance Department is a body of experts whose peacetime efforts contribute just as much to the safety of our nation as the wartime functions of the fighting units.

INDEX